You Believe In Jesus, Now What?

Steps to Following Christ

by Jeremy Vickers

You Believe In Jesus, Now What?
Steps to Following Christ

Copyright © 2018 by Jeremy Vickers
All rights reserved.

Book Design by Kelly Kloth
Graphic obtained through Pixabay

www.jeremytvickers.com

Printed in the United States of America

ISBN 978-0-9858034-1-4

Table of Contents

Dedicated to:

My Wife Jill

My Children

Mom and Dad

The people and pastors of Grace

Foreword

When Jeremy Vickers does anything, he does so with a well-thought out, straightforward plan. As long as I have known him, he has always been strategic and has a plan for him, a church, or a Christ follower that is easy to understand and a process to follow. The plan is always clear and makes sense to the participants included in the journey. Jeremy, though experienced in various forms of ministry, has now put his process for discipleship into writing.

Most churches are grateful for people to join the church, but they rarely move them from being a seat filler in a pew. I would be willing to say that most churches in America don't have a discipleship plan. The church understands that God meets us where we are, no matter where we are, but we have left out that God calls us to take steps to follow Him in the way of Christ.

In this book you will find a practical, biblically based plan to follow Christ. I am so impressed with this work that I am going to use it in the church I serve to orient new members to better serve the church and Christ. I would encourage every pastor in charge of, or wanting to develop a discipleship plan to use this book. Come up with your own questions for the end of each chapter. Create new membership classes to read and discuss it. Only good can come from it. The honesty of this book is what the church needs in this day and age. Thank you Jeremy for this approach and the want to grow Christ followers into disciples.

Buck Cueni-Smith
Senior Pastor
The United Methodist Church of Chillicothe, MO

Hallelujah, You Said Yes! Now What?
Introduction

One of my greatest fears as a pastor is that people would believe in Jesus, and not follow Him. Yes, pastors do have worries and fears. For many people who choose to believe in Jesus, it's easy to stand up and say "Yes, hallelujah, amen, I believe!" But then they go right back to their normal life. Some would say that wasn't really belief. Well, I'm not sure we can make that call. If someone says they believe, then we must take them at their word. How they choose to live their life after the public profession of faith is a whole other story. Deeds must follow their words, or they are considered hypocrites. But aren't we all? The Bible says, *"all have sinned and fall short of the glory of God"*- Romans 3:23. No matter how good we try and be, we will still struggle with sin. We have been set free and yet, we continue to make mistakes. We all can benefit from taking new daily steps to better our Christian walk.

This brings me to the reason for writing this book. What happens after we say yes? In most churches, there is no formal discipleship process. There might be some membership classes, home groups or others ways people might connect, but beyond that, there is not an intentional discipleship path for new or long-time believers. Yes, many churches say they have a path, but with infrequent worship and small group attendance, not many are following through on an abundant life with Jesus.

Churches do a fairly good job of helping people say yes to Jesus. We love to share and hear the words of Jesus in John 3:16. He said, *"For God so loved the world that He gave his one and only Son, that whoever believes in Him shall not perish but have eternal life."* Helping people choose to believe in Jesus is a pretty simple pitch. If presented in the right way, most folks will say, "Sure, I don't want to spend eternity in hell, why not believe in Jesus?" That is known as Pascal's Wager[1]. Basically, any reasonable person would choose heaven over hell. When presented with the option, most humans would choose joy over pain. If that was your only reason for becoming a Christian, you are missing out! Accepting Jesus Christ as your Lord and Savior has much bigger and wider reaching consequences than avoiding hell. You become a citizen of heaven and are called to help others come to know Jesus Christ. You have been set free from a life of sin, participate in the now and coming kingdom of God and spread the Good News of Jesus to the world.

I have observed many churches focused on drawing crowds, not making disciples. Most seminaries, if not all, do not train pastors how to make disciples. It's a buffet of different classes, mostly to help pastors become "theological" thinkers not disciple makers. A small handful of seminaries actually teach personal evangelism. If we take seriously the Great Commission, then our approach needs to change.

Then the eleven disciples went to Galilee, to the mountain where Jesus had told them to go. When they saw him, they worshiped him; but some doubted. Then Jesus came to them and said, "All authority in heaven and on earth has been given to me. Therefore go and make disciples of all nations, baptizing them in the name of the Father and of the Son and of the Holy Spirit, and teaching them to obey everything I have commanded you. And surely I am with you always, to the very end of the age."

Matthew 28:16-20

Moving from a John 3:16 "believer" to a Matthew 28:19 "follower" and disciple will not be easy. Christians have been trained to sit in their pews/chairs/metal buildings/stadiums and passively follow Jesus. We rarely go to Bible studies. If we do, they go nowhere. We serve inconsistently and frequently skip worship because other weekend activities are deemed more important. Let me say that again, many Christians frequently skip worship because other weekend activities are deemed "more important" than Jesus or worship. We believe, but we do not follow well.

How has the church responded to infrequent attendance? Worship has shifted from it's previous forms to uplifting and inspirational rock concerts, complete with smoke machines and brilliant lighting effects. So if people are bored, then feed their desire for edgy, fast paced and outrageous worship. Or, just throw your service online and a podcast. Maybe some people will watch, I mean worship. Full disclosure, the church I serve has online worship. It can be a great way to keep connected if you are unable to attend, especially if you are sick or out of town. It certainly was not meant to be a weekly replacement for worshipping with the gathered body of Christ, but for many homebound and caregivers, it has become a mighty blessing in their lives. This was a new learning for us and we are still learning the far reaching impact of online worship. We are still trying to figure out how to connect on a personal level with people that worship with us exclusively online. Some of them live in other cities, states and countries and have little or no connection to our broadcast campus. Ultimately, the church is the family of God. It's tough to be a family if we don't talk or see each other very much.

In the upcoming pages I will present down to earth ideas on how to be a faithful follower of Jesus. There are many books on how to evangelize, grow churches and lead relevant worship services. Brilliant pastors and leaders have filled that section with books and you would be well served to read a few of them. However, the discipleship section is rather bare, except for a few consistent and rather unnoticed voices. It's time for the church to remember our purpose again: to make disciples of all nations! This book is not a self help book for personal development. No, it's about the ups and downs of following Jesus every day.

Likewise, this is not a new church program to save the church. It's actually a call to accountability. We are called to practice what we preach. We say we believe then our words and deeds should prove it! Following Jesus requires a daily disciplined commitment. The Disciples spent three years following, learning and listening to Jesus. Some of us have spent thirty plus years in the church and have never invited anyone to worship. Rarely have we discipled a single soul to accept Jesus Christ as their Lord and Savior.

Whether you are a regular or infrequent church goer, new believer or long time Christian, please dive into each section with the passion of renewed focus on Jesus! Our faith can and will change the world if we actually walk the walk. Too few Christians take seriously their own personal discipleship. We can do and be better if we focus on changing a few small things every day. This book is not the end all be all of discipleship, but it will hopefully spark a new beginning for you. If you have accepted Jesus Christ as your Lord and Savior, this book will help you shape and form your new faith. This book is not about answers, but learning to walk the way of Jesus.

My prayer for you is that you press on to take hold of that for which Christ Jesus took hold of you. Hopefully by your example of Christian discipleship others may come to know the saving grace, mercy and love of God in Jesus. You will make mistakes, as I have, and every other Christian has as well. The mistakes will continue, but hopefully they will lessen as you grow closer to God. Be open to find your own connections to the stories, scriptures and teachings in this book. Dream a bit about how you might partner with God and the church in your own walk with Christ. I want to personally say thank you for taking this bold and courageous step.

Section 1- Believe and Choose to Live the Life

Chapter 1- You Believe In Jesus, Now What?!?

I grew up in a small midwestern farming community. As the county seat, my hometown branded itself the "Wheat Capital of the World". Essentially, we were known as the bread basket of the world as well. Interestingly enough, Jesus said He was the bread of life. So I really did grow up in God's country. There were numerous churches in town. We had Catholic, a few Baptist, Disciple of Christ, Lutheran, Presbyterian, Nazarene, Mormon and the First United Methodist Church.

As many families in small towns used to do, I grew up in church. My grandparents on my mother's side were Methodists. They went to church every week. They instilled the faith in my mom, which was then also instilled in my father, who did not grow up in a church going home. My mom sang in the choir, was involved in the United Methodist Women's group and volunteered in various other ways. In worship, my dad, my sisters and I sat in the back row of the church. That is truly the best place to sit in the church. Ask any Methodist, we can all agree on the back row! If churches charged for seating in the back row, no church would ever have a mortgage.

We went to church every week, unless we were sick or out of town. When we were at our grandparents, we went to their church. I was nurtured in the church and eventually was moved to accept God's grace and profess my faith openly. There were many wonderful Christians that helped me along my journey of faith. We also had some excellent pastors and leaders that led me down the path to salvation. I know I am richly blessed by the experience of others. I chose to accept Jesus Christ as my Lord and Savior and here is my story.

My Story

So there I was, sitting in my third grade Sunday school class. A portrait of Jesus hung on the wall to watch over our little class. Yes, that painting from the 1940's of Jesus, with the flowing brown hair, looking as if He was sitting for a portrait. Our teacher was reading from the Bible, teaching us about Jesus. I do not recall what passage she was reading. All was right in my little world. Then, she decided to upset the scene by offering a rather surprising observation. She told us that we were not truly Christians unless we invited Jesus into our hearts. My head immediately began swimming. Had I done that yet? My parents took me to Sunday school every week and I attended worship with them. We would go to church, have fellowship time, cookies and watered down punch, then everyone went to Sunday School. I also attended Vacation Bible School every summer. I had a little fold up paper church I would put money in and bring to church every now and then. After all that I still wasn't really a Christian? Yikes. I was afraid. What would happen to me if I died? Thinking back, I suspect our teacher might have been quoting Romans 10:9-10 which says,

"If you declare with your mouth, "Jesus is Lord," and believe in your heart that God raised him from the dead, you will be saved. For it is with your heart that you believe and are justified, and it is with your mouth that you profess your faith and are saved."

And one of my favorite passages in the Bible comes from John 14:23. *Jesus replied, "Anyone who loves me will obey my teaching. My Father will love them, and we will come to them and make our home with them."*

So, after church that day I went home and pondered what she said. Was being a Christian more than just going to church and

Sunday school? Was I not yet a Christian? After lunch and some thinking, I decided I better ask Jesus into my heart. Since there is no time like the present, and well, better late than never, I was going to do it. That afternoon I walked outside, because that is what you do when you are a third grader needing to talk to God. I stood near a corner of our house that had vines growing on it. It looked a bit like what I envisioned the garden of Eden would have looked like. I turned my eyes up to heaven and invited Jesus into my heart. There, I was a Christian.

I was saved. I signed up. I had my ticket to heaven and seriously, I was at peace. However, my public profession of faith came at the age of thirteen during the Confirmation service at our church. We all stood up and answered yes to Jesus! Many did so because our parents made us, some entered into the relationship half-heartedly, and others were already believers. The latter was me. I was already a believer because when I was in third grade someone said I should invite Jesus into my heart.

From the day I invited Jesus into my heart, I believed that I was a Christian and that Jesus was my Lord and Savior. God had made a home in my heart. Amazingly, since then I have prayed every day. I actually cannot remember a day when I did not pray. Prayer has covered my life with the grace of God. Asking Jesus into my heart began a wonderful and lifelong conversation with God. Conversation with God is just another word for prayer. When we pray, we do a lot of listening. Looking back, I feel deeply blessed by those who helped shape my decision. A Sunday school teacher spoke words of truth to my heart and soul and I was forever changed. Praying to God from a young age has significantly impacted the path I've taken over the years. My life has not been perfect, and I am a sinner, but my journey has been covered in prayer.

Not everyone has a memory of "that day." Some churches say if you can't remember "that day" then you are not a Christian. Respectfully, I disagree. Many people come to believe in Jesus gradually. It can be a slow, quiet conversation with Jesus that allows you to turn your heart and soul to Him. Everyone is different in their experience, and I would not question their walk with Christ. Lots of folks will accept Christ into their lives in a worship service. Others might have been reading their Bible and come to believe in Jesus. Still others will receive the gift of salvation while outdoors communing with God Almighty. For a few though, they will have been gathered together at summer camp.

Have you ever been to summer camp? No, not the summer camp portrayed in the culture, but a Christian summer camp on a camp site dedicated to glorifying God. For the last twenty years, I've counseled and directed summer camps for children and youth. I love summer camp! As a child and teen I also attended summer camp. It is potentially one of the most amazing spiritual experiences your children or youth will have in their lives. If you ask a group of pastors if they had a call to ministry or an affirmation of their call at camp, they will respond with YES! Camp can be a vision of what "church" should and could be for it's congregants. It's a little slice of heaven in 100 degree weather.

At summer camp we spend a week on a spiritual journey of discovery. We explore and experience God in new ways. At our camps, there are no pranks and other distractions to take our focus away from experiencing God in our midst. We have a weekly theme that allows children, youth and counselors to explore their relationship with God. We pray at all meals, we open the morning in song and launch into our rotations. We rotate between games, activities and Bible study. Of course there are hikes and swimming, but our goal is to not only have fun, but to grow closer to God. That means we ditched the Thursday night dance, talent shows and other events that distracted us from our purpose there.

Probably the highlight of the camp experience is evening worship. We bring gifted worship leaders, singers and a band in to lead worship. Our youth help lead as well. The children and youth are encouraged to participate in worship and many go home longing for a similar pattern to their daily life. When they arrive home though, it's back to reality. They go back to an over scheduled home life, school life and sports life. It all soon pulls them away from their growing relationship with God.

Perfecting the camp experience seems like a never ending battle and as such, we've made some serious changes to camp. Instead of focusing every night on altar calls and salvations, we emphasized consistent daily growth and each day and night build on a common theme. For those reading this who are big in the camp community, please don't close this book yet. There is a method to this madness of not focusing on salvations and altar calls every night. Why you might ask? Well, here is our why.

At many camps we gather for five to six days and we felt that a daily emphasis on the altar calls was a bit much for some folks. It's was a tough call because most of the kids at camp are Christians. They grew up in church and many are already baptized Christians. I grew up in the camp community and what I noticed as a young camper were children and youth who would go to camp, give their life to Christ and go back home and nothing would change. It was a momentary act that did not lead to a life long commitment. When speakers and preachers at camp would make us feel bad about our choices through a series of guilt ridden talks, some kids would woefully go forward and make a commitment that didn't always stick. I thought that when I had a chance to be a counselor or director at camp we would do things differently, so we did.

The last night of our camp we gather and receive Holy Communion. We are invited to confess our sins, repent of those sins and rededicate our lives to Christ. If someone is not a believer and came to church camp, hopefully they will make Jesus Christ their Lord and Savior! If not, we pray that in the future they would do so, but we do not pressure them during camp. None of us are perfect, and for sure we all make mistakes. Focusing on the momentary "win" of souls can discount and actually diminish the life long walk of faith in and with Jesus. The Holy Spirit was at work before the camp, during the camp and after the camp. Yes, if one soul is saved, there is rejoicing in heaven. Maybe this is more about the focus or intent of the camp we lead, but I would like to think all of us could see the differences here are fruitful and healthy.

After these children and youth would have their mountaintop experience, they go back home and nothing changed. They were asked to come forward, but not to actually learn how to follow. Many churches ask for a momentary act of commitment, instead of asking people to radically change their daily life and follow Jesus. It's easy to say yes in the moment, it's very difficult to continue to say yes every day. Let me pause here and say that if that method was effective and fruitful for you then amen. I however know that it does not reach everyone and we should be open to doing things differently. Just because the approach is different does not make it bad, unholy or wrong. The Christian community should be more open to our differences and celebrate them.

I know that many of us have experienced Christ in amazing and earth shattering ways at camp. Summer Camp is a revival for the soul of the believer, and can bring new people to Jesus Christ. But in my experience, it's certainly not a majority of campers, and again, without intentional follow up from a healthy and vital church, the kids will fall away. I do apologize if you are offended. I love camp, I love the camp experience, but I hope we can agree that we could do better.

How many times have you seen people become a member of a church, only to fall away? Without an intentional system of follow up and discipleship, we miserably fail the new believer. It's on us, not them. Conversion and transformation must be preached and people need to be received into the church, but without adequate follow up it might appear as if we care about the wrong things. Numbers should not count more than a lifelong Heaven sent disciplined life of following Jesus daily. We seem too often focused on the moment, not the personal journey.

Are you that person who came forward once and said, "Yes, I believe", only to fall away from the church and your relationship with God? If so, by no means, do not feel bad about it. Yes, you have some accountability in this, but so does the body of believers. As long as you can admit it, now you know. You know you need to change. You've known for a while now that your faith is not where it needs to be for you, your family and your church. Maybe a friend handed you this book so you could get back to the basics of the faith. I applaud you for actually making an effort with your faith. Not everyone takes their walk seriously with Christ. Now, it's time to repent of our past failure and sins and move forward to actually become a follower and disciple of Jesus Christ, not just a believer. Let's begin with some really basic stuff.

Confess and Repent

Confess and repent of your sins. Confess your sins directly to God and ask for forgiveness. Pour out your heart and soul to Him. Trust me, He's heard it all. By doing this you are letting go of all the sin and making room for Him. Confession is good for the soul. And going to a priest or pastors with your sins is not necessary. Do what you need to do to move forward. If you need to talk to a pastor, I'm sure your pastor has heard it all as well and will not judge you. Now you might be asking, what is sin?

Humanity has fallen from a state of righteousness and is now separated from God. The "fall" as it is commonly know is usually referred to as "original sin." There are two kinds of sin. There is Sin, and then sin. Big "S" Sin is usually refereed to as the rebellion of Adam and Eve. Think back to the garden of Eden. Ahh yes, paradise. Until Adam and Eve messed everything up by disobeying the will of God, they were living the life. The Big "S" sin is the original Sin that stains all humans from birth. Only through the grace of God in Jesus Christ can we find our way to God.

Then there is the other kind of "sin." They are the transgressions against God that we do every day. That would be willful disobedience to God, or denying God's divine will. The will of God is made known in the Bible, through teachings and the church. In the Old Testament, disobeying the Ten Commandments and numerous other rules decreed by God through His people were seen as sins. To know the rules and laws would help you better live a holy life, a life rejecting sin. If you sinned, there were some stiff penalties for such behavior. Again, sin is going against God's divine will.

Sin- Original Sin that Separates us From God

sin- Trespasses against the Divine Will of God

In their book Transforming Evangelism, Doug Powe and Hal Knight have a great definition of universality of sin as well. They say we are guilty and "responsible for all those thoughts and actions that are contrary to God's love."[2] If God is love, then when we act against love, we are rebelling against God. So then, we must self monitor every word and deed to ensure they are moving closer to the love of God, not further. Yes, this is a high standard, but it's a good guide for Christians. We can ask ourselves, was that a loving word or deed? If not, where did we go wrong? The love of God should fill our souls daily and motivate us to acts of mercy, service and personal holiness.

A final definition of sin is anything that moves you further from God. If we are to follow Jesus daily, things that move us away from following Him would be considered sin or sinful. The tough thing about sin comes down to sources of authority and the slippery slope of rationalizing our behaviors as holy and just, when in fact they could be sinful. Accountability from other honest Christians is important to your walk with Christ. We must be careful when evaluating our lives in the light of love. The world has a view on love, and it's not always consistent with the Christian and biblical view of love. Our journey of faith must be lived out in community, not per our own rationalized personally justified behaviors. Accountability is the key here. Your faith needs to be connected to the body of Christ in a tangible way so that through conversation, learning and worship you may be shaped and formed into a faithful believer and follower of Jesus Christ.

That is why the Christian faith was not designed to be done alone. We are better together and we are better in community. If you are not sure if your word and deeds are sinful, again, just ask a Bible study leader or pastor. They will be more than willing to chat. Talk to your other Christian friends. Be open to dialogue with others, and don't take offense at the opinions of others. Most folks are well intentioned, but may not always speak eloquently or compassionately.

As for sin, there are over six hundred sins or commands in the Old Testament and some say there are thousands of commands in the entirety of the Bible. Just search and you will find several different lists of sins. There are Old Testament lists, New Testament lists and lists of sins Jesus talked about in the Gospels. In my humble opinion, in the last thirty years, there has been more debate in the church about sin and what is a sin than in the entire history of the church.

Some Christians will say something is a sin, others will say it's not. They will all use the Scriptures and many other sources to cite why they are correct. In the Christian world we must be focused on the essentials of the faith like helping people choose to believe, follow and live a life of love in Jesus. Hopefully we do not allow the disagreements in the church to divide us. In other words, let's agree on the essentials, and then everything else should be worked out with fear and trembling.

Not only do we confess our sins, but we need to repent. Repenting of our sins is much more than saying we are sorry. It is the act of turning away from our sins. Repentance is not only acknowledging the sin with our minds, but turing away with our hearts and souls from the sinful behavior. Doing this requires a full commitment of your whole faith and you must want to change. If you do not you are doomed to continue to cycle back to those sins. That will keep you from being the person God needs and desires for you to be and will prevent you from truly living into the calling placed on your heart.

Rededicate

You need to rededicate your life to Christ, invite Jesus back into your life and commit your daily life to Him. To be a follower of Jesus Christ, we need to live a life of worship and praise. Our eyes should be fixed on Jesus in every thought, word and deed. If you choose to rededicate your life to Christ, do not do so half-heartedly. Put your whole trust and faith in His grace and mercy. You are choosing a brand new life in Christ, and letting go of your old sinful life.

When you rededicate your life to Christ you are acknowledging you are not where you need to be and need to change. That change only comes with action, not intention. We can have the best of intentions, but the road to hell is paved with good intentions. Your words must be followed by deeds. Look at the sins in your life and stop sinning. Get rid of them and move on. Do not look back, just set a direction and go!

Reconnect

We all need to live a life of prayer. One of easiest ways to begin this is praying the Lord's Prayer every day.

"Our Father, who art in Heaven, hallowed be your name. Thy kingdom come, thy will be done, on earth as it is in Heaven. Give us this day our daily bread. And forgive us our trespasses as we forgive those who trespass against us. And lead us not into temptation, but deliver us from evil. For thine is the kingdom, and the power and the glory forever. Amen."[3]

Memorize the Lord's prayer. It needs to become a part of you. Say it morning, noon and night. Trust me, once you begin to say the Lord's Prayer every day, your life will radically change.

Another valuable prayer that has helped me is the Jesus Prayer. Here it is:

Lord, Jesus Christ, Son of God, have mercy on me, a sinner.

It's short, sweet and to the point. In my daily prayers I begin with the Lord's Prayer, then the Jesus Prayer and then to my petitions and thanksgivings.

Petitions are requests we make to God directly on behalf of family, friends and those in need. There can be few, or there can be many. I include the chronically or gravely ill in my daily prayers. I also include family, others in need and the church. It can be ten minutes, or thirty minutes at a time. Oh, where do we find the time? We make time for the things we deem important.

Thanksgivings are simply saying thank you to God for all the blessings we have received. If you have received a hand written thank you card from someone, then you know how it feels to be thanked. God is no different. In offering thanks we acknowledge His work in our lives and we remember whose we are and who we are in Christ.

Finally, read your Bible every day. If you don't own one, download one. Many Bible apps have a reading schedule designed just for you. Read a chapter a day, or more. If you are not sure how to start, begin with the Gospel of Matthew and read it in the morning and the evening. Join a church Bible study. Follow a Bible study online. Do something to get into the Word of God! When you read the owners manual, you are a better steward of your life. You are being filled up with the Word of God and hopefully all the other unholy stuff just fades away.

Yes, I did not repent of my sins when I accepted Jesus Christ as my Lord and Savior. In the invitation of Jesus into my heart, I came to understand the nature of right and wrong, righteousness and sinfulness. I daily confess and repent of my sins, asking for guidance and help. The theology can be kinda messy, but so is life and so is the church. Now that you know all this, I pray that it will be helpful for you as you begin to follow Jesus daily and move toward a life of discipleship.

You believe in Jesus, now what?

Chapter 2- What Is A Disciple of Jesus Christ?

What is a disciple? A disciple is a student, follower and life-long learner of Jesus. They were deeply devoted to their teacher. Disciples listen, grow and act. They live the life. Are you a true disciple of Jesus Christ? Yes, you stood up somewhere along the way and said "I believe." Maybe you are born again. Wonderful! Hallelujah! Amen. You are a John 3:16 Christian. You have professed faith in Christ. But, are you a student, follower and life-long learner? Do you listen, grow and act? Are you living the life?

A disciple is a fully committed believer. They have moved beyond the Sunday morning and Christmas/Easter dance of many believers. They take seriously their faith and are attempting to grow daily in Christ. Their lives are organized around the call of Jesus and His Church, not organizing church activities around their busy schedule. In our culture today we see more and more distractions keeping us from living out the faith in a genuine and vital way.

The disciples were students of their Rabbi Jesus. Rabbi means teacher, disciple means student. Other common definitions include learner or apprentice. We know that Jesus walked around Galilee picking people to be His disciples. The Bible tells us they spent around three years learning from Him and witnessing the miracles and acts of mercy and justice. In the back and forth between Jesus and the disciples you can hear their hunger for understanding and knowledge. And when He asks them questions, which was rare, it's like final examine time.

In today's terms He would probably not be seen as a professor. Jesus would have been a combination of athletic trainer for the soul and the best preacher ever heard.

The Apostle Paul says to the Church in Corinth-

Do you not know that in a race all the runners run, but only one gets the prize? Run in such a way as to get the prize. Everyone who competes in the games goes into strict training. They do it to get a crown that will not last, but we do it to get a crown that will last forever.   1 Corinthians 9:24-25

What is an Apostle? An Apostle was someone sent on a mission or a messenger sent by Jesus to share the Good News. It also denotes the twelve disciples, and then Paul is referred to as an Apostle too. As they grew in wisdom and learning they were sent out. The Bible refers to the twelve Apostles numerous times in the Gospels. They had not fully completed their training, but they were ready to be sent out. A disciple was a student, and apostle was sent out to spread the message of the teacher.

A Coach, A Definition and the Team

Growing up in middle America, I had some amazing opportunities to play organized sports. One of my favorite sports was baseball. Every summer my parents would sign me up for little league baseball. We had uniforms, gloves and bats. It was fun. Over the years I played on several teams, usually sponsored by civic organizations. Investing in the lives of children in their community used to really matter and still does in some communities. They allowed a bunch of kids to enjoy the summer playing baseball, and all they asked was that our uniforms had their organization or business name on it. I played on several different sponsored teams during my elementary and middle school years.

As we entered middle school, I was placed on a team with two amazing coaches. One of them loved everything about baseball. He knew the stats of every major league player and could readily quote them. He was our baseball guru and we trusted everything he said. Our other coach was the dad of one of our players and I think he was in advertising. He would always have a good one liner or a way of looking at things that were meaningful and memorable. They were two of the best coaches ever.

If you know anything about baseball and kids, the one thing we all wanted to do was bat! We loved taking batting practice. The coaches would pitch to batters, while everyone else fielded. It was a true joy when you were able to rotate through the whole outfield, infield and stand at bat. Of course, that is not where our team began every year.

One of the most impactful experiences during the first few weeks of practice was that we were not allowed to hit a baseball. Why not? They were of the philosophy we should learn to crawl, walk and then run. The batters were given dowel rods (very thin piece of wood) and a wiffle golf ball. We would toss the miniature ball up and try and hit it. I know this probably sounds crazy, but if you can hit a wiffle golf ball with a dowel rod, your chances of hitting a 60-80 mph fastball are greatly increased. We were so fired up to hit, that when we actually had a chance, we made the most of every moment.

During our time with our coaches, they really taught us not only how to play the game, but how to practice the game. Among the many lessons they taught us, there is one major thing that still sticks with me to this day: They drilled into our brains the definition of hitting.

Hitting- **"The sequential unlocking of body parts to maximize bat speed at the point of contact."**

I'm not sure where they found it, but it stuck. If memory serves me correctly, it was a coach named Gary Ward who came up with the definition. It's probably not the exact quote either, but you understand. Hey, it was thirty plus years ago!

Our coaches helped us with the physical mechanics of the game by helping us learn about muscle memory and that it takes at least twenty-three days to make a habit or change a bad one. But, the learning that went on in between our ears paid off as well. We were so confident with knowledge and skill because we practiced well, we played without fear. We beat teams we should have never beaten, we stuck together, followed our training and won a bunch of games. By the end of it, our coaches didn't need to teach or coach us much anymore. We were well trained and ready to get out there and win games.

We should all be practicing Christians. Practice does not make perfect, but it helps us to grow and learn. Learning is a life long process. The journey of salvation is the destination for those who follow Christ. To be a faithful follower of Christ, we must practice the faith daily, not just on weekends or when we need it. When I think about definitions of discipleship and faithfulness, a few scriptures come to mind.

Love the Lord your God with all your heart and with all your soul and with all your mind and with all your strength.' The second is this: 'Love your neighbor as yourself.' There is no commandment greater than these."

Mark 12:30-31

Then Jesus said to his disciples, "Whoever wants to be my disciple must deny themselves and take up their cross and follow me. For whoever wants to save their life will lose it, but whoever loses their life for me will find it. What good will it be for someone to gain the whole world, yet forfeit their soul? Or what can anyone give in exchange for their soul? For the Son of

Man is going to come in his Father's glory with his angels, and then he
will reward each person according to what they have done.
Matthew 16:24-27

The Disciples

There were twelve disciples: Peter, James, John, James, Simon the Zealot, Matthew, Philip, Bartholemew, Judas, Thaddeus, Andrew and Thomas. Judas betrayed. Peter denied. Thomas doubted. John and Matthew wrote Gospels. They were all supposedly ordinary men that were called into extraordinary circumstances. Through their discipleship and the way they followed Jesus, billions of people know about Jesus Christ. If they did not carry the message of Jesus, nothing would have ever been known about the peasant King from Nazareth who came back from the dead.

To be candid, not much is really known about the disciples. We know what the Bible says about them and it's sparse at best. There are numerous authors who have woven together a wonderful tapestry of the little scraps we know about them. A larger picture of how they were perceived by religious leaders can be found in the book of Acts.

When they saw the courage of Peter and John and realized that they
were unschooled, ordinary men, they were astonished and they took note
that these men had been with Jesus.   Acts 4:13

They were uneducated, mostly blue collar workers, from a small region called Galilee. None of them were extraordinary, special and were not skilled or trained orators, which makes their testimony and witness much more powerful. Speculation about them runs wild among scholars and locals in the Holy Land. A few years ago I traveled throughout Turkey and learned there are three graves to

Mother Mary. Folklore was also built up around the disciples as to their final resting places as well.

In the Gospel of Matthew we take note of how quickly they chose to follow Jesus when He asked them to "follow me". They were young Jewish men who said yes to following a Rabbi. He became their teacher and they became His students. Were they waiting for the Messiah? The Messiah would come to restore Israel and reign as King. Prophecies about the Messiah are scattered throughout the Old Testament. The disciples probably knew the prophecies and when offered a chance to follow this obviously well schooled Rabbi, they said yes. The immediacy of their response causes us to wonder if they knew more about Jesus that it appears. Although, it might have just been a big honor to be picked as a disciple of a Rabbi. Either way, they chose to follow.

If they knew the Scriptures well, they might have been able to interpret the signs and say, "hey, there is the Messiah". Sadly, my generation became the first biblically illiterate generation in the United States. We can't quote the Bible and we don't know many of the stories, parables or teachings. Christian education in the 1980's and 1990's miserably failed us, and we failed it too. There are few large Sunday school classes these days. The majority of churches struggle with discipleship, especially with small groups. I pray God helps us with the next generation.

One of the ways in which the church would train disciples was to memorize Bible passages. I knew Christians who could quote or recognize a Bible passage on hearing just the first few words of the first sentence. Alas, today that is rarely true. There are too many translations, people are too busy and distracted to even think about relevant Bible passages for their lives. The vast majority of Christians would struggle to quote a passage of the Bible, but we can quote song lyrics and movies perfectly. It is very difficult to remember the word of God when our hearts, minds and souls are full of worldly things.

There are several passages in the Bible we should memorize and carry with us. One I find helpful is Matthew 28:19
Therefore go and make disciples of all nations, baptizing them in the name of the Father and of the Son and of the Holy Spirit.

The Disciples followed Jesus for three years. They soaked up His knowledge, wisdom and teachings every day. They hung out with Him, learned from Him and followed Him. They witnessed amazing miracles and saw Jesus demonstrate extraordinary compassion to the least, the last and the lost. Jesus showed them how God truly viewed sin and the "righteous." He called them to "follow Him", repent and "believe in the Good News." He helped them understand how to deal with temptation as well. Every Christian will be tempted and as far as we know, most if not all of the disciples were tempted too.

Can you imagine giving up your livelihood to follow a small town preacher? The disciples left their homes, families and jobs to follow Jesus. We don't know the full back story on them, so maybe they knew Jesus or of Jesus when He called them. When they were in school they might have played on the same baseball team, or whatever sport they played back then. We can't really know the history Jesus and the disciples might have had, but we know when they were called they followed. It wasn't just belief either, it was actually following Him day by day for three years.

Temptation

During my elementary school years, I lived in one of those idyllic neighborhoods where just about every house was filled with a family and kids. As a kid, there were plenty of neighbor friends to play with and we did. Our neighborhood was brimming with kids my age. One street over were just as many kids. We would play outside until dark when our moms would call us back in for supper. At the time we were all considered to be "good" kids. No bullies or troublemakers in our neighborhood, just kids looking to have some fun. No worries or fears about strangers either. We would be outside, unsupervised for hours on end.

One of my buddies that lived down the street had an older brother that was into dirt bikes. His brother had a relatively small motorcycle for motocross. He had the outfit, the gloves, the helmet and the bike. My friend and I were warned to never touch his bike. My friends mom also warned us to never touch his brothers bike. Of course, we know what that means. When no one is around, touch the bike!

So, late one morning my friend's mom was out shopping and his brother was asleep upstairs. My friend and I snuck outside and rolled the motorcycle into the backyard very quietly. We aimed to ride that thing across the backyard. With no one around, we could be daring and tame this beast. My friend said I could go first and so I did. I sat atop this mechanized beast and my buddy showed me the clutch, how to start it and how to rev the engine. No need to shift, as we were just riding around the backyard. No need for a helmet either, or gloves because they wouldn't fit. As I sat there contemplating how cool this would be, I had this nagging thought that "this might not be a good idea". I knew this was wrong. I knew the right thing to do, but I chose to do the wrong thing.

As we fired up the motor, put it in gear and I slowly let out the clutch, it began to move forward. I then gave it some gas and it took off. This would be my first and last ride on a motorcycle. Again, as I moved forward the "not a good idea" moment had taken hold of my heart, soul and mind. It was not fear, it was the realization that I had been told not to ride this, but I did anyway. I had no idea what I was doing.

Ultimately, that is what we would describe as sin. Doing something we are not supposed to do is sinful. Honor thy mother and father of a friend? No. Respect your elders? Nah. "Steal" someone's motorcycle? We borrowed it! Was it a sin against God to take the bike? Here is where the daily life of the Christian and the Bible collide. Remember, sin separates us from God. Sin is going against the divine will of God, not holding ourselves accountable to the love of God and moving further from God. In the light of all those things we can agree we were not supposed ride the bike and when we did, we did not honor his mother or father. Technically, we stole the bike from it's rightful owner, even though we were going to return it. To commit a sin is the act of rebellion against God's divine will. We committed two sins right there and we had intentions to lie about it if we were caught.

Rationalizing of sin in this world is at an all time high. If we can justify our behavior by parsing or using word olympics, then we do. Riding a motorcycle in itself is not the sinful act. It is the willful disobedience against God that is the sin. Children learn at a very young age right from wrong. All wrongs are not sins. But we sure do try and make all wrongs sins. Is it part of God's divine will to disobey parents? No. What if they are in the wrong? There we go again picking winners and losers and justifying our behavior.

Followers of Jesus Christ do not make excuses for sinful or bad behavior. They have been well trained in the ways of Jesus and have chosen to live the life of a disciple. That means, there are no excuses. If you sin, repent, move on and then stop sinning! Do not dwell on your past or your mistakes. Repent and move closer to Jesus. We all make mistakes, few of us move on from them.

Even the good or the righteous make mistakes. We do not intentionally choose a path of sin or recklessness. The life of a disciple is one wholly focused on Jesus Christ. The focus on His teachings, message, transformation, love and compassion is on the tip of every disciples tongue. We breathe out the joy and hope of the Good News in all that we say and do. Once we accept Christ and move closer to Him, there is a feeling that we all get when we begin to walk down the path of sin again. It's a nagging sense of things not being right. It's a voice that says that what you are about to do is not a good idea.

As the motorcycle streaked across the backyard I had a horrific realization. I did not know how to stop this thing. I did not know where the brake was and as such, the chain link fence at the end of the yard was coming up very quickly. I was only in first gear but that engine was revving loudly and I was moving fast. Not knowing what to do, I could have froze. But for some reason, and to this day I have no idea why I did this, I grabbed the clutch. It disengaged the gear and I was no longer speeding across the yard, I was slowing down.

The motorcycle crashed into the corner of the fence. There was relatively little damage to the bike or the fence. I sat there balancing the bike unable to move. My buddy came running down to me, followed by his brother yelling at both of us. His brother had heard the engine start up. As I dismounted the powerful bike, I leaned it over to my buddy. I then disengaged the clutch again, and the back tire starting spinning in the grass. His brother thankfully grabbed the clutch, and then turned the bike off.

We thought we might escape punishment as the fence was not damaged and his brother wasn't going to tell because he left us unsupervised. That was not the case. There was a giant bare spot in the yard from where the tire had peeled out while bike was pushing up against the fence. Yes, we were busted. Moms and dads were involved and we were grounded. The scene of the crime could not be hidden or explained away. We had done something wrong and it could not be denied. Oh, and by the way, we didn't even consider wearing a helmet. Why be safe when you are being bad?

Flee the evil desires of youth and pursue righteousness, faith, love and peace, along with those who call on the Lord out of a pure heart.

2 Timothy 2:22

A believer, follower and disciple of Jesus Christ knows their core purpose is to make disciples of Jesus Christ, baptizing in the name of the Father, Son and Holy Spirit. And when someone comes into the family of believers, we are also supposed to be *"teaching them to obey everything I have commanded you…"* Matthew 28:20.

Who's team do you want to be on? Team Jesus or Team sin? It is so easy to pick Team sin. Early on, it seems like an easier path to walk. With Team sin, there is a lot of lying, hiding things and deceitful behavior. Eventually, it all comes into the light. To pick Team Jesus means we've learned to be a believer and follow Christ. We have also learned how to avoid sin. A disciple of Jesus Christ loves the Lord our God with their heart, soul, strength and mind and loves their neighbor as themselves. They are devoted to the teachings of Jesus and reject the evil powers of this world. Disciples know that this world does not have the last say and that eternal life is a free gift from God, but we must choose to receive it. Disciples believe…

Apostles' Creed

I Believe In God The Father Almighty
Maker of Heaven and Earth
And In Jesus Christ His only Son our Lord
Who was conceived by the Holy Spirit
Born of the Virgin Mary
Suffered under Pontius Pilate
Was crucified, dead and buried
On the third day He rose from the dead
He ascended into Heaven
And sitteth at the right hand of God the Father Almighty
From thence He shall come to judge the quick and the dead
I believe in the Holy Spirit
The holy catholic church
The communion of saints
The forgiveness of sins
The resurrection of the body
And the life everlasting. Amen.[4]

To define discipleship we turn back to our baseball definition of hitting. Discipleship would then be the unlocking of your spiritual life in Jesus to grow in faith, hope and love and share the Good News. The focus is not on getting to Heaven, but on reaching others in the name of Jesus. Our goal on our journey of faith cannot be focused solely on our salvation and life, it must be focused on helping others find Jesus. We cannot do that if our lives are distracted or focused on sin. What knowledge do we as followers these days need to soak up?

Do we know the Scriptures well enough to see the prophesies of the coming Messiah? I would encourage you to pour over the

Scriptures daily so you may better come to know Jesus, His disciples and the body of Christ.

When our lives are focused on following Jesus, we tend to avoid heading down the wrong roads. If you are headed down a bad road, hit the brake. Don't go down that path. It's not healthy, it's not good. If you have learned the definition of discipleship, you can rely on that focus to fight off all the sins that continue to pull us away from the Gospel. A pupil, student, learner and apprentice of Jesus Christ knows the way to go. They may not always choose it, but as they grow closer to Christ, the choice becomes clear. Choose to follow Jesus daily. Resist the temptation to chase after the world and be a disciple of Jesus.

Chapter 3- Choose the Path of a Disciple

There was an early training manual for followers of Christ. It was known as the Didache. It means teaching. You can find a few different copies out there, but to sum up the teaching is rather easy. It begins by giving followers of Jesus Christ a very simple choice. You can choose to follow the way of the world, or the way of Jesus. It actually says, "there are two ways, one of Life and one of Death, and there is a great difference between the two Ways"[5].

We are all on a path. We are going somewhere. Every person has an eternal destination. But while on earth, we need to choose a path. The driving force for the path can be one of a myriad of things. Some choose their path based on the hopes and dreams of others. Or we choose a path because of family, career, education, health, social or economic status. Honestly, some never choose a path. They just drift through life being blown back and forth by the wind. They might wonder, is there something more to this life?

In the Gospel of John, Chapter 14:6, Jesus says,

"I am the way and the truth and the life. No one comes to the Father except through me."

Is Jesus your way, your truth and your life? If not, and you have accepted Jesus Christ as your Lord and Savior, it's probably time you made Him those things.

I've had a few jobs throughout my life. I've been a paid furniture delivery guy, baseball and tee ball coach, worked construction, multiple internships, office clerk in charge of data input, Christian educator, youth minister, associate pastor, pastor and lead pastor. Each one of those jobs has significantly shaped my life and my path. When we are young, maybe high school aged, people begin to fill our heads with all kinds of notions about the future. You might have been asked, "What do you want to be when you grow up?" My favorite response from a friend is, "I will tell you when I grow up." He's forty-three years old. Not sure when he will grow up, if ever.

One of my first "jobs" was working construction. My dad had hired young high school aged me to drive five and a half hours to Texoma, Oklahoma and pull aluminum siding off of a house so the house could be completely renovated. We agreed on the pay and I would be able to take all the aluminum and recycle it to make some extra money. Back then, recycling paid well. So I was all in.

Young high school aged me did not know the way to Texoma. Growing up in a small town, I had not driven more than thirty miles away from home. This was a bit further. Since it was such a drive, I would follow my dad out there, we would stay in a hotel, I work for two days and then come home. The old 1980's beat up blue pickup truck would hopefully carry me out there safely. If it didn't, my dad would be right there to help me.

We started out in the morning on our trip and arrived in the early afternoon. I had a few hours of daylight, so I put on my tool belt and went to work pulling this old, worn out aluminum siding from the house. The tool belt consisted of a hammer, some nails and a screw driver. It was a more of a nail pouch with the hammer hanging on for dear life. For the task at hand, there was one huge problem. I had no idea what I was doing. There was no manual for this stuff. The house was huge and it was going to take me a few days to pull the siding off, and then load it into my truck. As I stared at the wall I wondered where to begin.

My dad was talking to the home owner's son Randy, who was a mountain of a man. He was well over six feet tall and weighed three hundred pounds. They both walked over to me, I wondered out loud where to start the deconstruction. Randy asked if I wanted a little help. Again, not knowing what I was doing, I welcomed the help. Randy stepped up to the house, reached down and grabbed the bottom row of siding. He began to pull and walk back away from the house while holding the siding. I heard the nails begin to pull away from the house. The wall of siding remained locked as he pulled more and more of the wall down. The nails continued to making popping noises until eventually he was standing about twenty feet from the house and whole wall of siding came crashing down to the ground. He said, "seems pretty easy to me." For him it was. However, the rest of the siding around the house did not come down quite as easy for me.

I spent around two days pulling the siding down, picking up nails and loading the aluminum into the back of the truck. After lunch of the second day I was beat and ready to rest. Although, I was young and full of energy so when my dad suggested I head back home with my load of siding and I agreed. I was ready to go. There were lots of things to do and people to see back home. Life is short! My dad then said that he had a few more days work out there and I would need to drive the five and a half hours back home in the beat up old blue pickup truck by myself. No safety net, no one leading me and back then, no mobile phones. He simply said, "you know the way home."

One of my favorite passage in the Bible is the calling of the twelve. When Jesus begins to call the disciples, the Gospel of Matthew recounts it this way:

As Jesus was walking beside the Sea of Galilee, he saw two brothers, Simon called Peter and his brother Andrew. They were casting a net into the lake, for they were fishermen. "Come, follow me," Jesus said, "and I will send you out to fish for people." At once they left their nets and followed him. Going on from there, he saw two other brothers, James son of Zebedee and his brother John. They were in a boat with their father Zebedee, preparing their nets. Jesus called them, and immediately they left the boat and their father and followed him. Matthew 4:18-22

Once called, they immediately left their families, their jobs and all they knew to follow Jesus. They gave up the path they were on to learn, follow and listen to Jesus of Nazareth. They let go of their worldly lives to follow Jesus. It wasn't a slow debate with family and friends as to what was the right course of action. As far as we know, they did not talk to their family, spouses or friends. Matthew clearly states, *"at once they left their nets and followed him."* They gave up the life they knew for the promise of a better life with Jesus.

There is no, "sorry dad, we are going to go follow this fella for the next three years." No apologies. No excuses. They just followed. It makes me wonder what we need to give up to follow Jesus. Are there things in between us and following Jesus? Would some of those things be career, sports or entertainment? Have we placed a higher priority or certain things in our lives than following Jesus?

Imagine it, your children go off and follow some small town Rabbi who preaches repentance and salvation. This Rabbi speaks of the afterlife, temples being destroyed and challenges the normal religious order of things. Wouldn't it be quite bizarre to see them chase after him? What about the thousands of followers He accumulated over a three year ministry? For those who shy away from trends, the popular and what's hip, you might have missed out on the real deal.

Choosing to believe in Jesus is one thing. Following Him daily is a whole other thing. It's a head and a heart thing, it's internal. Following the path of a disciple of Jesus Christ is putting foot to ground and moving forward. It means a conscious rejection of other paths to pursue the path of Jesus. There will be some habits and relationships you need to let go of, so that you may more closely follow Jesus Christ

These guys left their livelihood, their families and jobs. There is great security in just keeping things the same. If you have a stable, safe job, why would you ever take a chance and leave for something else? Aren't we all told from a young age to play it safe? Why try, push or fight for something different? Because it's a calling. A calling beckons you to a different life, and in Jesus Christ you find new life.

Before the disciples are called by Jesus, a sometimes overlooked event happens, recorded in Luke 4. Remember Luke is where we find the the birth of Jesus recorded. We all read Luke's version on Christmas Eve and Christmas day services. A few short chapters after the birth story, we find Jesus grown up and in His hometown. He goes to the synagogue in Nazareth and these events are recorded.

Jesus returned to Galilee in the power of the Spirit, and news about him spread through the whole countryside. He was teaching in their synagogues, and everyone praised him. He went to Nazareth, where he had been brought up, and on the Sabbath day he went into the synagogue, as was his custom. He stood up to read, and the scroll of the prophet Isaiah was handed to him. Unrolling it, he found the place where it is written: "The Spirit of the Lord is on me, because he has anointed me to proclaim good news to the poor. He has sent me to proclaim freedom for the prisoners and recovery of sight for the blind, to set the oppressed free, to proclaim the year of the Lord's favor." Then he rolled up the scroll, gave it back to the attendant and sat down. The eyes of everyone in the synagogue were fastened on him. He began by saying to them, "Today this scripture is fulfilled in your hearing." Luke 4:14-21

I wonder if any of the disciples or their parents were there during this event? If so, a Rabbi getting up and proclaiming such things would cause a big stir. People possibly talked about this and it would have spread quickly. Since Rabbis' would have disciples and as far as we know Jesus had not picked any yet, people would be really talking and speculating. Anything involving anyone in a local church that hints of scandal spreads like wildfire. Sadly the church continues to struggle with gossip.

Maybe the idea of this Rabbi inviting people to follow Him and then immediately doing so is not so far fetched? Maybe to us today it is, but not during the time of Jesus. Although when someone in the church asks someone to help you can say no, but when the "senior" pastor calls and asks, it's a lot more difficult to say no. A Rabbi functioned not only as a religious teacher, but a mentor and guide for his disciples. They were placed in his care and charge such that they could grow and learn in the Word of God.

I heard the other day to be successful in any field of endeavor you need two things. First, you need a great mentor. Second, you need drive. A mentor would be someone to show you the simple basics and fundamentals of your field. They also help you along the path by answering questions and gently guiding you. Although, mentors are not always gentle. You can learn from their knowledge and wisdom, especially if you actually listen to them. Mentors can take an interest in your future and help you learn and grow. The mentor or teacher of the disciples was Jesus of Nazareth.

MENTORS

I've had some absolutely amazing mentors in my life. In most professions, there is a mentoring process, formal or informal. You are hired, put under the direction of someone and you become an apprentice. Somewhere in the future you learn enough to move up. Then you move up again and eventually you are mentoring new people. Interestingly though, most were not "assigned" to me as a mentor.

As mentioned in chapter 2, baseball played a big role in my young life. Our coaches were not just coaches, but mentors for life. We learned many life lessons as we played and practiced together. My coaches always had a great way of framing life and baseball.

One summer I was struggling to hit the ball. My batting average was down, as was my on-base average. One of my coaches pulled me aside and asked what was going on. He said I had too many strike outs and would need to move me from lead off batter if I didn't improve. I had been doing great at the beginning of the season, so something must have changed. We discovered, as we lost a few games in the middle of the season I was trying to swing for the fence more and more. Instead of getting on base and letting the other guys hit me in, I was trying to win the game with every swing.

Coach said, "we would rather have you walk than get a hit. We need you on base. And don't swing for the fence, hit the ball on the ground like we taught you." Too many of us swing for the fence, instead of just trying to get forward momentum. I took his advice and ended up reaching base 8 out of 10 times by the end of the season. He was essentially teaching me to be a part of a team, be patient and know that we don't have to go it alone. This is something I have continued to learn over and over throughout my life. There are days we need to swing for the fence, but not every day. Being patient is a virtue.

I found my second mentor in my late teens. I worked on a construction crew with a couple of guys. I was the youngest and most inexperienced, but most of us were new hires, so we all got along pretty well. Our boss was a health nut, work out freak, body building entrepreneur with a great small construction business. He was always on the grind looking for new business. He was also a perfectionist when it came to the job. If it didn't look right, we had to do it over again. Two stories come to mind about work ethic and quality of work when I think of him.

My coworker and I were putting in windows and siding on one wall of an older house. We'd been on the wall most of the day. Just as we started to put siding above the windows our boss came to inspect our days work. "Windows look good. You guys need to teach me how to do those good and fast." My co-worker could pull an existing window and have the new one in and set in about fifteen minutes. He was good. As the boss continued to inspect our work, he started backing away, further and further. Then he stopped, tilted his head and said, "Pull it down. It's not hanging right." We tried to disagree, but as we stood where he stood, we could tell, it was a bit off.

Often times in life you can be working a problem, and be so focused on it, you forget to take a step and look at if from a different perspective. Sometimes it takes someone else helping you see the mistake. Here is the best part of the story. Neither one of us were mad. We were paid by the hour. So our unintentional mistake would cost us no money. Our pay would not be docked for our mistake. We just needed to fix it.

I learned a lot during my time with "the boss." He was a good Christian man that demonstrated the love of Jesus in word and deed. His family reflected Christian values and they would often speak about how to raise Christian children. They would visit him on the job sites. He also was a great story teller. He recounted stories of high school football games, sporting events and family gatherings. The boss also took us to a variety of restaurants for lunch, and fortunately, back then, he paid. But there is another story the sticks out in my mind that I carry with me.

Working outdoor construction means that you are at the will of the weather. Construction in snow and rain is not fun, but doable under the right circumstances. In Kansas during May, June and July, you always have your eye on the sky for those pop up thunderstorms. That year we had our fair share of thunderstorms, hail storms and tornadoes. In others words, we had missed a few days of work.

One beautiful Kansas mid-morning, we were working on ladders putting up soffit and facia. We had been pushing hard to finish the job in the next few days, and we were tired. The boss knew it, so he was right there with us, on the same wall, out working us. I found that when someone can set a pace faster than the others, oftentimes others will speed up, not always catch up, but work a bit harder.

Next to the house was a series of railroad tie four foot raised bed gardens. Working on ladders is not safe. It has to be done with care. The boss on this day was a bit careless. He slipped off his ten foot ladder and landed on his rear, up against the raised beds. His neck and head hit the top railroad tie, and his arms turned out and he went limp. We raced over to him to see if he was alright.

Boss opened his eyes, and slowly stood up. We looked at him and said we should probably knock off for the day. He was not having any of it. "Let me go sit down for a bit." He sat in his truck for about twenty minutes. Both of us kept peering over at him to see if he was still upright. Finally, he came walking over, crawled back on the ladder and went to work. No run to the ER, no concussion protocol and no call to the insurance company. Just a few sips of tea and back to work.

I've known a lot of folks who work farms, construction and other tough jobs. Injuries happen quite often, but rarely do docs or nurses treat them. They just keep going about their day, working hard to make a living. That work ethic is something I feel should be instilled in most every Christian. Push through the spiritual pain and keep working for Jesus. Not every day is full of sunshine, some days are cloudy. But the Son is always shining so keep working on your faith.

Why? We all have excuses to not follow through on our commitments. Whether you skip reading your Bible, forget to pray or treat others rudely, you need to push through the distractions. Our faith should drive us down a path of discipleship. Having good mentors to keep us on task is vital to our future faithfulness. Being a disciple of Jesus is hard work. You will constantly be growing and changing as you experience God in new and miraculous ways. Do not let your faith become stagnant and remember to focus on your larger purpose of sharing the Good News.

The final mentor I would like to share with you was assigned as a mentor through the church. He was a young church start pastor full of passion, drive and excitement. He never stopped moving and always had an interesting turn of phrase. His church start had gone from four people to four hundred and fifty in about eight years. Impressive. His passion and work ethic were extraordinary. He could out work and out evangelize just about any other pastor.

In one of the assigned meeting times, he pulled a bunch of us young clergy together. He grilled us and challenged us to begin to think about what kind of pastors we would be and how we would cultivate a life of fruitfulness. His passion was church starts, and it was evident in every word and deed. He loved the church and wanted to reach people for Jesus Christ.

The gathered pastors were not sure if they wanted to plant a church. I did not want to plant a church. I did not feel called to it. As we spoke up, he was surprised no one wanted to plant a church. I said, "I want to go into dying churches and turn them around." He nodded and said, "that's hard work, maybe even harder than planting." He did not discourage me from pursuing that calling, although he did ask a few more times about planting. Eventually, when given the opportunity, I was given a few chances to turn around dying or closed churches. I deeply appreciated him as a mentor and church leader.

He would always remind us to stay on mission and have a plan. When or wherever we gathered, he was constantly giving us books and encouraging us to read. "Leaders are readers" he would say. "If you're gonna lead, your gonna bleed". Some thoughtful phrases for future leaders. He has continued to guide and lead others to discern their call to ministry and challenge them to passionately and faithfully pursue the calling God has placed on their hearts.

DRIVE

If a great mentor is the first thing you need to be successful in your chosen vocation, then the second thing you need is drive. Drive is an innate motivator that gets you up in the morning. It helps you take on the world for a cause, purpose or desire. Another word for drive would be passion. Passion helps you focus on the loves of your life. You are what you love.

In my hometown there was a guy who had a local barber shop. He had a pretty good business because many fathers and sons would come to receive a haircut. He told great stories and was good at connecting with people. When kids and teens would come to see him, he would treat them with the same respect as he did the adults. This made a big impact on us because he talked to us during haircuts just like he would our dads. Sometimes kids can feel as if they are better seen than heard, but our barber made us feel welcome.

In my teen years the barber was cutting my hair and he made a remark that has stayed with me all these years. He said, "your dad has more drive than anyone I've ever met." As a young man, it was good to hear another adult speak well of my father. Take note reader, it's nice for children to hear their parents spoken well of by other adults, especially when the parent is not around. Take note men, speak well of your wives in front of them to others.

Anyway, for one reason or another, my dad is a hard worker. He has worked six days a week for almost all of my life. He often would be gone two to three days a week for work, but always made it back for my Friday night football and baseball games. My dad's passion and drive came from the desire to provide for his family and better himself. He was always competing and challenging himself to do better.

That drive for life is something that is inside us, pushing us to work and grow. It can be trained and learned. This year my dad turned seventy years old. He is still working six days a week, partially out of his desire to stay active, mostly out of leading a disciplined life. We spoke recently that he might go back to five days a week so he can spend more time at home, with grandkids and with mom.

Jesus said,

For where your treasure is, there your heart will be also.

Matthew 6:21

If you treasure something, you will focus on it. When you love God and neighbor, you will spend your life offering love to them. If you love the world, you will chase after it. Your thoughts, words and deeds will be focused on whatever you truly love. The disciples loved God, and came to know and love Jesus Christ. Although one of them chose to love money and the world, and became known as a the betrayer. His name is synonymous with betrayal. He was known as Judas. To follow Jesus you need to learn the way, truth and the life. That means you pay attention to His teachings and life. We must surround ourselves with His other followers to help keep us accountable to His way. But, after all the following and training, there are moments when we need to step up and stand out among our family and friends. When that moment of arrives, will you be prepared to walk the walk? We have a saying in our church. We help people meet Jesus, walk with Jesus and make it home. Do you know the way to bring others home?

Let's return to my Texoma story. When my dad said "you know the way home", I was not excited to be out on my own. Most people spend their lives wanting to grow up too soon, move out of our hometowns or just get away from the authority figures in our lives. Few of us are prepared for the responsibilities of life. Everyone is in a hurry to grow up and move on, instead of realizing the blessings they have around them. We have precious few moments with our parents. Listening and learning from them will end some day, so take the time you have left and cherish the relationship. If they have already gone to be with the Lord, cherish the memories.

I started the five and a half hour drive back home. I'm glad to report that there were no speeding tickets, blowouts or struggles of any kind, other than only having an AM radio in the truck. It was rather uneventful by the standard of the world, but for me it was pretty worrisome and stressful. So many things could have gone wrong, but I did know the way. I even stopped at the same gas station we had stopped at on the way out. I knew the way because someone showed me the way.

When you choose the path of a disciple you are choosing a well traveled path. Many have traveled down the same road, why not choose to learn from them? Honestly though, too many Christians try to go it alone. They say, "I'm gonna do it my way", only to end up in trouble, needing rescue by others. I assume someone suggested you read this book and they might be praying for you and your journey. Who knows, maybe they want you to be better connected to them and the body of Christ.

I would like to share one final thought about your future. The church I currently serve has a preschool. At preschool graduation we ask the kids what they want to be when they grow up. The responses are oh so cute and often comical. Most of the children will pick the job of their parents. We often hear they want to be a: firefighter, nurse, teacher, pastor, doctor, etc.

One particular statement made us chuckle a few years ago. A young girl was graduating from preschool and was asked, "what do you want to be when you grow up?" Her response, and I quote, she said "Nothing!". She laughed and then ran, actually loudly stomped across the wooden stage to receive her diploma. Her twin brother said the same thing right after she did! Hilarious.

In all the years I've never heard any child, or adult for that matter, say when they grow up they want to be a faithful disciple of Jesus Christ. Why would they? We focus so much on career, that we miss out on life. At the end of your days, do you think you will look back and wish you worked more? Hopefully not. No, we would probably wish we spent more time with family, or made a more positive impact in the world. Instead of looking back late in life with regrets, choose today as the day you change your path. Stop making excuses and focusing on the wrong things, pick today and say "I will follow the path of Jesus."

Every one of my mentors had passion and drive. They were all Christians as well. Along my journey of faith there are countless other Sunday school teachers, preachers, youth pastors and others that have deeply impacted my journey of faith. Even if it was only for a few months or years, their words of kindness, patience and example have allowed me to learn from their mistakes and seek to be a faithful follower of Jesus Christ. I pray you find good mentors with drive. They are all around us, we just need to be willing to listen and learn. When Jesus called the disciples, a few might have been skeptical. Don't let your skepticism or cynicism keep you from learning or following.

It's time to take the next step beyond belief and move to a life of following Jesus. Trust the teachings of your mentors, because they know the way. Stay out of the ruts you have made for yourself because they only keep you stuck and spinning your wheels. Choose to be a new creation in Jesus. Be the person God calls you to be and witness to His grace, love and compassion to the world. Find some great mentors, or be open to them finding you.

Section 2- Follow Jesus

Chapter 4- Fix Your Eyes on Jesus

Do you not know that in a race all the runners run, but only one gets the prize? Run in such a way as to get the prize. Everyone who competes in the games goes into strict training. They do it to get a crown that will not last, but we do it to get a crown that will last forever. Therefore I do not run like someone running aimlessly; I do not fight like a boxer beating the air. No, I strike a blow to my body and make it my slave so that after I have preached to others, I myself will not be disqualified for the prize.

1 Corinthians 9:24-27

A few years ago my wife and I traveled to Yosemite National Park. It was an extraordinary and deeply spiritual experience. Yosemite is often called "God's outdoor cathedral." Yosemite is one of the most beautiful and inspiring places on earth. You need to go! As you enter Yosemite you see waterfalls cascading gently down the rocks into valley streams. Up next to the waterfalls, you can hear the roar of the water and feel the full force of it's power. It is mesmerizing. If you have been to Yosemite you know this and you also know you will see wild bears roaming around. We saw a least six bears in our first twenty-four hours and several more throughout the week. Bears are apparently everywhere in the valley.

On our first day driving through the Yosemite Valley we saw some beautiful little bear cubs playing near a log. It was about fifty yards from the road, up an embankment. We slowed the car down and pulled off to the side of the road. We stepped out and walked back up the road toward the bears, brand new DSLR camera with long lens in hand. This would be something we could talk about for years to come. It was a perfect little scene.

We walked slowly and quietly, and fortunately no other cars passed by us. Around seventy five yards away I started taking pictures. These two cubs were playing and rolling around, and we had big smiles on our faces. What a beautiful sight to see in Yosemite. Our hearts were completely full with joy. Then in an instant, it all changed. Mama Bear came up quickly behind the little bears and put her massive paws on the log. I continued to take pictures. We were around fifty yards away at this point. She then looked directly at us, slapped her paw on the log, dragged her claws across it and roared! Our eyes became the size of saucers and we turned around and ran!

Wait, "you did what?!?!" you are asking. We ran. As we ran the thirty yards back to our car my lovely and brilliant wife said, "I thought you aren't suppose to run from bears." My response, "I know, but I'm running!" as was she.

No matter how much training you have, or how much you think you know, none of us can tell how we will react in these kinds of situations. Fear can take over. I have been in a few situations where fear did not take over. I kept my cool and led others out of harms way. You just never know how you will react until you in the midst of it. Sometimes, despite all of our training, how we define ourselves and who we think we are, we fail and just run.

And let us run with perseverance the race marked out for us, fixing our eyes on Jesus, the pioneer and perfecter of faith. For the joy set before him he endured the cross, scorning its shame, and sat down at the right hand of the throne of God. Consider him who endured such opposition from sinners, so that you will not grow weary and lose heart.

Hebrews 12:1-3

The letter to the Hebrews was possibly written by the Apostle
Paul. The letter encourages believers in the midst of their struggles
to persevere and follow through on their faith. Some of them might
have been under such difficult persecution they were considering
renouncing their faith and returning to their old ways. Have we
ever felt that way? Yes, we have all felt like giving up.

No matter who we are scrutiny and pressure are difficult to deal
with, especially if it continues over a period of time. Some people do
thrive under pressure, but many struggle. Here Paul encourages us
to not give up and to persevere by running the race that has been
marked out for us. What does he mean there?

God has a plan for our lives. It is not a moment by moment plan
of a puppet master. However, God has a path for us to follow. The
path is set forth by living a life when we fix our eyes on Jesus. There
is a final destination prepared for us and a narrow path to follow.
He is the author and perfecter of our faith and when we
unabashedly follow Him, we live a life of abundance and joy. His
example of living through hardship gives us hope for the trials to
come, knowing we are not alone and we can endure with and for
Him.

We are encouraged to consider Jesus and His sufferings so that
we will not grow weary and lose heart. Do not lose heart. There are
so many things in this world that disappoint us. You may be
reading this now with sadness and disappointment in your heart.
Remember, you are not alone. The church cares for you. Seek out the
church and find comfort, direction and peace with them. If at first
you don't succeed in finding a church that fits, there are numerous
churches around all of us, if we are willing to go to them.

In our lives, we will find ourselves in unfamiliar and uncertain
places. Just like our bear story, even if you think you know the way

to go, fear can grip your heart. Many things will make your heart jump in fear. These days for me, it's rare, but it still happens. Here are a few things I've heard others share over the years. These will make your heart pause for a few moments.

- waiting to hear your child cry when they are born
- a doctor who says "it's cancer"
- your dad had a heart attack and needs a quadruple bypass
- the company is eliminating your job
- a spouse wants a divorce

Much of life is us just waiting to hear good or bad news. Bad news comes, as rain falls on the righteous and unrighteous. So if we are sad, hurting and lost, I direct you to a Bible passage that brings me comfort.

One the most amazing chapters in the Bible is John 14. You might have heard it read at a funeral, but you need to read it for yourself. It covers it all. Jesus is spending time with His disciples and He knows He won't be with them much longer, so He lays it out for them. In thirty-one short verses, you can hear the care and love He has for them, and the encouragement He offers.

Do not let your hearts be troubled. You believe in God; believe also in me. My Father's house has many rooms; if that were not so, would I have told you that I am going there to prepare a place for you? And if I go and prepare a place for you, I will come back and take you to be with me that you also may be where I am. You know the way to the place where I am going." John 14:1-4

Jesus has prepared a place in Heaven for believers. It is there, and you have assurance of it. This is not based on your worth or good works, but the work of Jesus on the Cross and His resurrection. You do not need secret knowledge and it's not based on what church you attend. No, it's because He cares for you and loves you. He says *"believe in God; believe also in me"*.

He then goes on to say that we will be where He is going. Amen! Hallelujah again! We are on a journey of salvation that brings peace and purpose. Our place is secure in Heaven and between now and then we celebrate a life of faithfulness in Christ. We worship, pray and serve. Our lives are no longer ours, we are servants of the most high God. Don't be fooled by the hucksters who tell you doing and giving more will help you receive blessings or abundance. You choose the life of a disciplined disciple as a response to His grace, not to earn His grace.

"If you love me, keep my commands. And I will ask the Father, and he will give you another advocate to help you and be with you forever— the Spirit of truth. The world cannot accept him, because it neither sees him nor knows him. But you know him, for he lives with you and will be in you. I will not leave you as orphans; I will come to you.

John 14:15-18

Jesus continues here with explaining that if we love Him, then we should try to keep His commands. Wait, what? Try? No, it simply says "keep my commands". Remember His commands to love God and neighbor? That's it. Yes there is more to being a Christian than those, but it sums up the message of Jesus. Love God, love your neighbor and love your enemy. Do we really love Him if we can't keep those commands?

He promises the Holy Spirit to be with us. You mean we have a spiritual guide leading us? Yes. The Holy Spirit, the least explained and written about person of the Trinity, is inspiring and gifting the church. The Holy Spirit guides, leads and sustains the body of Christ. We are led by listening and praying. The call placed on your heart is nurtured by the Holy Spirit. Be sure to always listen and be ready for God's revelatory message every day.

Jesus goes on to say He will not leave us as orphans. We are not abandoned, although possibly persecuted and suffering, we are not alone! The plague of loneliness that many experience does not need to be endured again. With Jesus and the Holy Spirit, God tells us in every way possible that we need not fear and we are not alone. The epidemic of loneliness is cured by the church. When we are deeply connected to the body of Christ in worship, small groups and mission, we are set free.

"All this I have spoken while still with you. But the Advocate, the Holy Spirit, whom the Father will send in my name, will teach you all things and will remind you of everything I have said to you. Peace I leave with you; my peace I give you. I do not give to you as the world gives. Do not let your hearts be troubled and do not be afraid.

John 14:25-27

Jesus repeats Himself to reiterate that we are not alone and the Holy Spirit is with us. We have the Holy Spirit with us and the darkness will not win. When you have Jesus in your heart, you never need to walk a path of loneliness again. God will guide us with every step that we take. We just need to listen.

Mission Trip

A few years ago I was leading a mission trip of teens and adults home from Window Rock, Arizona. We had visited the Navajo nation and spent a week building, working and serving the local community. If you've been on a mission trip you know that drive home can be a long one. After sleeping on a floor and eating cold meals, we were ready to go. Knowing that, we charted a different route home to keep things interesting. As we did that, God had an experience before us that we would never forget.

Our travels home took us through mountainous Colorado. I had never been through Colorado and never driven through the mountains. On one side of the road was a mountain, and the other side was a massive three hundred foot drop. Making the trip in fifteen passenger rental vans was not a great deal of fun. But, we traveled slowly up the mountain, with most everyone asleep.

As we rounded a curve, there was a small truck up ahead that seemed to be having problems. It was coming down the mountain toward us and the trailer it was pulling was swaying back and forth. Suddenly, I saw the back tire of the trailer shoot off the road in front of us. The trailer pitched to one side and pulled the truck over and it began rolling down the road directly at us. I slowed the big van down and pulled over to the side, nearest the cliff, praying the truck and trailer would stop rolling. The van behind us also stopped.

The truck came to a rest in twenty-five yards in front of us. It had flipped about ten times. I looked at the guy next to me and said, "we need to go check on them." I then said, "kids, stay in the van". We exited and yelled to the van behind us to watch our kids and call 911. It seemed to take forever to traverse the space between us and the overturned truck. We had no idea if anyone had survived.

The truck was on it's side so I jumped up on top of it and looked down through a smashed passenger window. A hand reached up and I grabbed it. Jim stood in front of the of the windshield looking to see how many were in the truck. I asked how many were in the truck. "I can't tell" he said. "Jeremy, there is gas leaking out of the truck" Jim said. A woman's voice said "just us." Then we heard it. A baby cried.

My heart began to race. I was unable to open the door on top. They would not be able to climb out. I was still holding the wife's hand and I looked at Jim. I shrugged not knowing what to do. No one else was around but us. I let go of the hand and said we would be in shortly. I jumped down with Jim and pointed to the windshield. Jim dug his fingers into the top of the windshield and ripped the glass out. He would be puling out shards of glass from his hands for the next six months.

I helped the husband out, Jim carried the wife out and we heard a woman's voice as she rounded the truck say, "I'm a nurse, I can help." I grabbed carseat with baby still strapped in and handed her to the nurse. We gathered in the grass away from the truck. By now multiple people were calling 911 and a tragedy had been averted. Everyone was in shock. As more gathered, we quietly walked back to our vans and drove away.

We drove in silence for miles until someone broke the silence. It was one of our teens with a deeply profound opinion. He said, "Uh, that was pretty cool." What he meant was, it was cool that we were there to help and we did. "But for the grace of God go I" was on a loop in my head. I truly believe we were there for a reason. What are the chances that at that very second, that moment we happened by that location? And where did that nurse come from? God did not cause it to happen, but He was with us in the planning of the trip, the mapping out our journey and the timing. When we bring God into our daily life through prayer and listening, He leads us to the places where we can be most useful.

God did not cause the tragedy, but His people interceded into the world of struggle, tragedy and heartache on His behalf. Sometimes we listen and sometimes we don't. I've found we often do not listen when we are overly concerned with the affairs of this world. There are natural and human-made tragedies every day. It's how the church responds in the Spirit that shows where our hearts, minds and souls are in our walk with Christ. The Holy Spirit guides us, will we follow?

To finish my Yosemite bear story, we obviously made it. We ran to the car, jumped back in and locked the doors. Only then did we look back to see mama and the cubs had left too. Our hearts were pounding in our chests, and we were out of breath. We managed to agree that it was a good thing we made it, and we would not put ourselves in another situation like that again. We didn't, well, not for another two days when we had a bear follow us on a hike through Hetch Hetchy, but that is another story for another time.

I'm not sure what bear is chasing you, but with Jesus, your fear need not cause you to stray from the God ordained path before you. His calling is mightier than the molehill you are facing. In Jesus we can defeat our fears and worries. That does not mean we won't face heart pounding scary situations, quite the contrary. Most of our faith can be summed up in how we react to things in this world. We are not perfect, but in Jesus, we are saved. That assurance and confidence causes us to react differently than the rest of the world. We do not react in fear or worry, but in faith and hope.

Chapter 5- Thoughts, Words and Deeds

A farmer went out to sow his seed. As he was scattering the seed, some fell along the path, and the birds came and ate it up. Some fell on rocky places, where it did not have much soil. It sprang up quickly, because the soil was shallow. But when the sun came up, the plants were scorched, and they withered because they had no root. Other seed fell among thorns, which grew up and choked the plants. Still other seed fell on good soil, where it produced a crop—a hundred, sixty or thirty times what was sown.

Matthew 13:3-8

Over the past few years my wife and I have planted a garden. We started off rather small with a few tomato plants, peppers and cucumbers. It's grown over the years with an average of over two thousand tomatoes from our now rather large five thousand square foot garden. You might say it is a bit out of hand, especially the years when our kids were born.

Starting out while dating and our early marriage, we grew our garden at my house, which eventually became our house. I had never grown a garden before, but it seemed to impress my future wife that I was willing to let her grow a garden in my backyard. I went with it and was hooked. We began with a modest sized garden near our back fence. A tiller, which we borrowed from my parents, broke open some soil and helped us plant the first year. Eventually, we ended up growing most our own plants from seed. This adds a whole new level to gardening. You begin in February and March preparing soil to grow the seeds in. We utilize grow lights and a small rack we purchased from the hardware store. Around Mother's Day we plant our summer garden. The soil outside is tilled a few times before we actually plant. We plan out our garden on a map to best maximize our space. If you are going to scar the earth you better have a purpose. We normally till two to three times before planting, and then at least once after harvest.

The yield at our old place was ok, but nothing spectacular. We were happy with what we received, but over time the soil just didn't seem to produce like it once had. We also had a few years of drought which caused a shorter season. This went on for about eight years. We were happy with what we had as we expanded, but knew it could be better.

Fast forward to our second home with a three thousand square feet garden our first year, and expanded to five thousand square feet of garden our second year. We added a bunch of extra plants into the mix for our garden. We now grow over two hundred tomato plants, two kinds of sweet corn, cucumbers, squash, peppers, okra, turnips, lettuce, radishes, onions, and it horrifies me to admit this, but my wife grows kale. We did so well we signed up to sell at the local farmers market! That was on our life goal list and we checked it off with great joy. We freeze and can much of the produce and use it between growing seasons. A significant portion is also given away to family, friends and those in need.

The interesting thing we learned as we moved is that the soil at our new place is much better than our old house. The soil out here is amazing. However, there is one spot that is not so great. The previous owner had a garden as well, and when we plant where he planted it just doesn't grow well. It's ok, but not great. You may not know this, but it's not only the seeds, sun, rain or fertilizer that makes your plants grow, it's your soil. If the soil is out of balance it will not yield good or great results.

At both places we sent in our soil to be tested. The University came back with interesting results. At both places, we needed to add certain things to the soil to balance it out, and once balanced, it could grow better. Now, being that we are amateur gardeners, our attempts to balance out the soil has not always worked well. In other words, after growing a garden on the same spot for 8 years, there was not much we could do to reproduce those early results with out adding a bunch of top soil and organic material.

At our new place, we learned that rotating crops and planting a cover crop, while leaving one spot of dirt out of rotation, can significantly change the future of your garden. Farmers do this all the time. My wife grew up on a dairy farm and my grandparents had cattle and crops. My grandfather won several conservation awards during his time farming. It's in our ancestry to grow things and to take care of our property. So, we have started rotating crops, planting cover crops and taking one area of the garden out of season for a year.

Finally, we compost. This is not easy in our society today, but very worthwhile. We currently have two compost piles in our yard. With as much biomass coming off our gardens, we need to return it to the soil. We think the best way to do that is by composting. Essentially, certain kinds of organic material is mixed with leaves and grass clippings to slowly decay for six months or longer, then is tilled back into the soil. I heard a speaker a while back say that if every family in the USA would compost and grow a small garden, the refuse into our land fills would be decreased by 50%. Not sure about that number, but it gives some of us a goal to move toward.

Why tell you all of this? During the time of Jesus, many of his family and friends lived a more agrarian society. They lived off the land. The season's mattered not just for the joy of change, but you can lose crops if you plant too early or too late. Timing is everything when planting.

Jesus gives the disciples an explanation of the parable of the sower.

"Listen then to what the parable of the sower means: When anyone hears the message about the kingdom and does not understand it, the evil one comes and snatches away what was sown in their heart. This is the seed sown along the path. The seed falling on rocky ground refers to someone who hears the word and at once receives it with joy. But since they have no root, they last only a short time. When trouble or persecution comes because of the word, they quickly fall away. The seed falling among the thorns refers to someone who hears the word, but the worries of this life and the deceitfulness of wealth choke the word, making it unfruitful. But the seed falling on good soil refers to someone who hears the word and understands it. This is the one who produces a crop, yielding a hundred, sixty or thirty times what was sown." Matthew 13:18-23

We can plant the word of God all over the world, but no roots, persecution and the rocky places will keep it from growing. When scattering seed, shouldn't we be careful when and where we plant His word? Why waste your time in places it won't be received as easily? To understand where God is sending us means we are listening to God. God speaks to us every day, are we listening? Where do we need to plant and do we go ahead and plant in places without good soil?

We should spread the word of God everywhere we go, but should not be upset, discouraged or frustrated if we go to the wrong places and fail. It does mean we can't scatter seed in those four different soils, but know that it won't always take root and grow. Go to the difficult places and share the word, your yield will not be as good, but you never know when it will take hold. This is a special calling by too few.

So, where are you planted? In the good soil? If not, move to the good soil. I've been in many churches throughout my life and honestly, not every church will fit you. A few years ago on the weekend after Christmas I shared a message about finding the "right" church. Not everyone will like everything about their church. Sometimes the church does not get along. I truly and faithfully believe that God has the "right" church for you. It is a place that will feel like home and a place where you feel you fit. If you are not in the right church for you and your family, find it. It's out there and it's up to you to find it.

After the message a Baptist preacher on vacation came up and introduced himself. He said, "I've never heard another preacher encourage people to go to another church if they didn't feel they fit where they were." He was encouraged that we were not in competition with each other. We are on the same team and we should all help build the kingdom of God. Sadly, some churches and Christians are not as committed to this as others.

Networking is big these days. Everyone in business is encouraged to be in professional networking group and to have learned how to network. Networking is interacting with others to our mutual beneficial ends. Computers networked together can become quite powerful. Certain kinds of trees only grow where two or three others are planted. Pastors are often encouraged to join civic organizations to help reach new people for Jesus Christ, and to also make a positive impact for our communities. Not all networking is positive or works, but the attempt at connecting and building relationships is helpful. We should not look at every relationship as either positive or negative. If it's not beneficial to us, we don't just walk away. Our faith needs to be impactful in the lives of others. Life cannot revolve around only our wants, needs and desires. How might it look for you to join a group and make an impact and plant a few seeds for Jesus?

Back to our garden. Four things have significantly hindered our garden over the years. They are walnut trees, bamboo, animals and bugs. Walnut trees are not good for tomato plants because they will stunt their growth and keep them from bearing fruit. They give off something called juglone. Essentially, it's poisonous to tomato plants. Most people say keep your tomato plants about twenty-five to fifty feet away from walnut trees. Some folks suggest even farther. Walnut trees will also keep peppers, potatoes, eggplants and a few other vegetables from growing.

No matter how much we pray, tomatoes just cannot be planted next to walnut trees. We could plant hundreds of potatoes around a walnut tree and they would not grow. The best gardner in the world could plant every kind of pepper plant and they would not grow if they were too close to a walnut tree. No matter how hard we work, the amount of books and research we do or the amount of money we throw at a garden, tomatoes, peppers, potatoes, eggplants and a few other plants will not grow near a walnut tree.

The Bible says,

Do not be misled: "Bad company corrupts good character."

1 Corinthians 15:33

Is there someone in your life that keeps poisoning your faith? There is some question in the church as to how we reach out to sinners. Jesus shows us that we should eat with sinners and invite them to new life in Christ. The problem for many of us is our faith has not developed enough to witness to those living far from the path of God. That means that when you go hang out with those of bad company, they may move you further from God instead of you bringing them closer to God. If you surround yourself with negative, break you down types of people, they will break you down.

This does not mean you can't be friends or acquaintances with non-believers. It does mean that you better be ready to stand up for what is good, right and just. Believers of Jesus Christ are not always well received in our culture. In fact, some folks are down right rude and mean to believers because they do not fully know who we are or what we believe. The church has been horribly misrepresented by those who do not know us. Some churches have learned, don't go it alone when proclaiming the good news. That is good advice.

Bamboo. Dear Lord, please remove from me my frustration and bad memories of bamboo. When I moved into my first house many years ago, I did not take note of the interesting looking bush in the back yard. I was a single guy who found a raised ranch house with a high ceiling living room, centered around a large windows and a fireplace. I loved that house. However, the previous owner had worked at a local garden supply company. For some reason, they planted three plots of bamboo along the fence.

When you plant bamboo, which you should never do, it will take over everything. It does not spread quickly, it takes root like you would not believe. It's a nasty, noxious vile plant that will make your life miserable if you let it. We spent three years fighting with that stuff as we attempted to clear an area for a garden. We thought we had removed it all, then more would come up.

I spent hours digging out the roots. My wife spent hours cutting the bamboo shoots down. My wife is tough. She grew up the youngest of six sisters on a dairy farm. They also had crops and cattle. You may not fully understand the massive amount of early morning and late evening work a small dairy farm requires. It's a lot of tireless work that makes you weary. Even she succumbed to frustration against the vile plant.

As I relayed this story, an acquaintance shared with me this advice. "If you find a bamboo plant on your property, get rid of it. Then go find the person that planted it and punch them in the face." I'm not one for violence, but I now understand the level of frustration in that statement. After years of battle, we did finally remove most if not all of the bamboo.

Now we turn to the animals and bugs. Deer like our garden. They really like sweet potatoes. Young deer will come in an eat the flowers from them, which then means the potatoes will not grow as big as they should. They also will take a big bite off the top of corn stalks and they really like turnips too. Deer like our garden. I like watching deer in the back yard, but we've taken to non-toxic and non-lethal ways of keeping them away. Our methods do not work well, and honestly, we let them enjoy the Vickers family garden buffet. As for the raccoons that destroy our corn, well, I don't like watching them walk around, and neither do our neighbors. Lots of motion activated lights and talk radio at night have kept them away.

Finally, the bugs. My goodness, the bugs. From aphids to Japanese beetles, we have fought the good fight for the good of our garden. We don't like to use pesticides, so we've gone to some other methods to protect our garden, one of which is going out twice a day to check the squash leaves for new squash bugs. It seems like a never ending battle against bugs that like the fruit of our labor.

We are not farmers or ranchers. We are backyard gardeners. I can't imagine the pressure on our farming communities these days. Small family farms are disappearing. As the world changes so will the soil. I pray for the farming and ranching families who continue to try and make a healthy difference in our world. Pray for those who feed you and provide for one another.

Why do we keep planting a garden with all the things that seem to be against us? I haven't even mentioned the weather. There have been years when very little rain falls, and then some years May and June has "higher than average" rainfall, whatever average means anymore. Of course who can forget the long dry July spells when our tomatoes really need rain. Wind can also whip a tomato to death and well, it's a bit windy here in the area. At least we don't live in western Kansas because the wind there is outrageous.

We plant because we plant. It's who we are and what we do. Both our families have farmers in our background and back yard gardens. It's passed down from generation to generation. It also teaches us a lot about life and how God works in the world. It's no different with the faith. We are called to plant.

The Bible is full of passages about planting and building up, not tearing others down.

Do not let any unwholesome talk come out of your mouths, but only what is helpful for building others up according to their needs, that it may benefit those who listen.   Ephesians 4:29

With every thought, word and deed we are cultivating something. Are we cultivating a life with God or a life built on the world? A life built on the desires of this world will lead you down a path of misery, sadness and destruction. The life of a disciplined disciple is one of plowing, planting and working to see fruit appear. It doesn't always produce fruit, but we pray it does.

In talking with the disciples about believers, Jesus sets forth a way of discerning who is a true believer and who is not.

"Watch out for false prophets. They come to you in sheep's clothing, but inwardly they are ferocious wolves. By their fruit you will recognize them. Do people pick grapes from thornbushes, or figs from thistles? Likewise, every good tree bears good fruit, but a bad tree bears bad fruit. A good tree cannot bear bad fruit, and a bad tree cannot bear good fruit. Every tree that does not bear good fruit is cut down and thrown into the fire. Thus, by their fruit you will recognize them. Matthew 7:15-20

You will know them by their fruit. The world will know us by our fruit. They will know us by our love as well. I ask again, what are you cultivating? Are you growing in the love and knowledge of God or are you a consumer of the culture? It is a daily battle to flee from temptation, but one worth fighting. Don't be a false prophet for God. In the church we do lots of spreading the Word of God and often it seems like the seed did not take hold. But remember, the kingdom of God is not a sprint but a marathon. It takes time for the Word to grow in someone's heart, soul and mind.

Let your thoughts, what you dream and hope about, be filled with the Word of God. May God's vision be clearly revealed for your life and family. Every day we all must choose to live the life of a disciple or not. Some days, you will fail. There will be days when your thoughts, words and deeds do not match your faith. It's called sin. Now, that does not give you permission to sin. It is an acknowledgment that sin can be a daily struggle. And when we admit that, it allows us to enter into His presence with an honest faith seeking guidance, not self-praise.

Peter reminds us to focus on what truly matters.

Therefore, with minds that are alert and fully sober, set your hope on the grace to be brought to you when Jesus Christ is revealed at his coming. As obedient children, do not conform to the evil desires you had when you lived in ignorance. But just as he who called you is holy, so be holy in all you do; for it is written: "Be holy, because I am holy."

1 Peter 1:13-16

To be holy means we have let go the sin that pulls us away from God. The daily steps we take move us closer to God, not further. Every moment of every day we must be devoted to serving and praising the Lord. We often talk at our church about not giving up a Sunday. In the life of the church there are Sundays that don't have the same energy and attendance as others. No matter how many people "show up" to worship, we still go all out for Jesus. Don't give up a day, even if you are weary and tired, and don't give the devil a foothold. Rest on the Sabbath, but don't give it up.

James says,

As the body without the spirit is dead, so faith without deeds is dead.

James 2:26

Let your faith be something that is alive and growing. Be planted in the good soil of God so you may grow and reach out. Bask in the light of the Son and be filled with living water that brings a wellspring of salvation and hope. May your thoughts, words and deeds be completely and wholly focused on Jesus. Cast off the fears and desires of this world and be planted firmly in and with the church. Bloom where you are planted!

Please permit me to make a suggestion. No matter where you live, you can have a garden. It can be a patio tomato, window herbs or a raised bed garden. The earth will grow things if you work it. You will learn a lot about the world and how things grow by simply trying to grow a garden. Soil matters as does the sun, water and weather. And who knows, by growing something you may be able to give some of it away. A conversation and relationship may be sparked by the simple gift of your garden.

Chapter 6- Serve Someone Else

Date Night!

One of the first dates my wife and I went on before we were married was to a soup kitchen. Please re-read that line. I said, "let's go on a date to a soup kitchen." Not really. However, when we began dating I thought it would be good for her to see what I do. I'm a pastor. I lead a church that is focused on serving those in need. We have several mission programs to serve the poor and those in need. One of mission programs feeds around one hundred and fifty people. It's a month meal at a soup kitchen.

Our church has been working with this particular inner-city soup kitchen for over twenty years. So why not take my new girlfriend on a date there? We signed up to help. That Saturday we arrived to help prepare the meal at our church. Volunteers spend a few hours working with other families in the church. Of course there was a natural curiosity about who the pastor was dating. So our team was a bit larger that weekend.

After the meals are prepared, we drive to the soup kitchen. We set up the food, the kitchen and the room. Then the doors are opened and a flood of people come in. We met many homeless people and encountered a few homeless families there. Thankfully where we serve is not just a soup kitchen. They provide assistance to help people get back on their feet again and find employment. Several training programs are also offered. Our small part of taking care of a meal helps free up resources for them to help more people.

It was a rather memorable date for both of us. We spent time together and we made a difference. Since then, we have led others to help serve as well. Two other locations inspire us to serve again and again. They allow you to sign up online and serve families of children in the hospital. At both of them, it also means serving a meal. No spaghetti or leftovers. Our favorite meal to serve is homemade chicken and noodles, mashed potatoes with butter and sweet corn. The food that sticks to your ribs provides some sustenance to families in need or crisis. We give our best and that is who we are called to be when we embody the kingdom of God.

Jesus and Service

In the Gospel of Matthew, we read some of the most amazing words about mission and service anywhere in the Bible. Jesus had been telling parables and using metaphors to explain to the disciples the "kingdom of Heaven". He then shares these words to drive home the point and purpose of mission.

"Then the King will say to those on his right, 'Come, you who are blessed by my Father; take your inheritance, the kingdom prepared for you since the creation of the world. For I was hungry and you gave me something to eat, I was thirsty and you gave me something to drink, I was a stranger and you invited me in, I needed clothes and you clothed me, I was sick and you looked after me, I was in prison and you came to visit me.' "Then the righteous will answer him, 'Lord, when did we see you hungry and feed you, or thirsty and give you something to drink? When did we see you a stranger and invite you in, or needing clothes and clothe you? When did we see you sick or in prison and go to visit you?' "The King will reply, 'Truly I tell you, whatever you did for one of the least of these brothers and sisters of mine, you did for me.' Matthew 25:34-40

"Whatever you did for the least of these, you did for me." For some this might be seen as a checklist of missional behavior. One might point to this and say, "you didn't do this one thing, so you are not a good Christian." There are only a few places in the Bible where you truly see a checklist and this is not one of them.

In this passage Jesus is summing up His teachings on the kingdom of Heaven. As He does, we see a clear explanation of two paths here on earth. He even distinguishes between the sheep and the goats. The folks that will be welcomed into the kingdom have offered hospitality, helped and cared for the stranger and others. It's an attitude of mission, not a list of righteousness. Maybe what you treasure is where you heart will be...

Do you care about those listed here? What about others? It's easy to love those who love us and to care for those we know, but what about those that feel estranged from God and far from the church? Who cares about them? And the "far" from church and God language can be problematic when we realize that God is everywhere and has come near. But, there are folks that have walked a path away from God which means their self defined state of being would be far or estranged from God, specifically from our perspective of closeness to God. Knowing that we then realize our spiritual journey cannot just be about us making it to Heaven. There is more to life than just your inheritance of fire insurance.

Mission Trips

A few years ago I led a large group on a mission trip. We traveled across the country to help renovate a church that had been burned down by satanic arsonists. Yes, you read that correctly. The church was being rebuilt by volunteers from across the country. Teams were organized and a flow chart of tasks was then checked off after a team would finish. The new building would be five times as big as the original church. Amen!

When you work on mission sites often, you realize that there are many well intentioned, good hearted people in the world. The reason I say well intentioned is because the skills and execution don't always match the measure and kindness in their heart. On many trips, skilled labor teams will spend a few days "fixing" the mistakes of other groups. Sometimes it takes a few days to notice those mistakes, but eventually they are found out.

On this particular mission trip the church needed several thousand square feet of insulation installed. So, most of our team worked morning to late night putting up rolled insulation in the basement. It took days. If you've ever messed with insulation, you will know that it is not a "fun" task. But, it was next on the list and our crew of youth and adults joyfully went to work. They donned hats, gloves and masks and knocked it out! Great job team. And the local women's group from the church fed us really, really well. Amen.

The other issue at hand was fiber cement siding on the back of the church. The wall was over fifty feet high, and nearly thirty feet wide. Somewhere along the way as the siding was applied, the measurements were off from side to side. When they reached a few windows in the middle of the wall it became painfully apparent that it did not match up. It looked dreadful. I have no idea how long the mistake sat on the back of the building. I also could not forecast how long it would continue to stay up there until a professional showed up to fix the mistake. We could ignore it and pray the next team would take it up, or we could tackle it ourselves. Being that I had spent the better part of a decade learning and hanging siding on houses, we decided to fix the mistake.

This was precision work, since we were twenty-five feet up in the air. It was not easy, as our "unskilled" labor force of youth needed to be trained quickly because the trip was only a week long. Fortunately, I had several highly skilled adults to balance out our passion vs. skills. In two and half days, we had the wall running true and were able to move above the windows and set up the next crew for success.

Our trip was a wonderful experience of hard work and impact making life changing mission. We helped move the project along and we all learned a lot about working with each other and teamwork. I love mission trips. It creates and environment for serving, learning and sharing. One of my big rules on mission trips is that we work every day, and on the final day, we have a big day of fun! Meaning, six days of work, and then a day at a theme park or huge local attraction. If you are going to serve, make it count.

During our particular trip we encountered another youth group on a different kind of mission trip. They had rented a huge bus to take fifty of them on a mission trip. They spent two days on site working, and then the rest of their mission trip was spent at a theme park in Florida. Needless to say we were shocked. Most of their time was to be spent an expensive park, not in mission. They said this was their last trip with their youth director and they wanted it to be memorable. For who? The church? The people we were serving? I'm all for fun, but not at the expense of mission. For those who didn't realize it, in the Methodist church mission means service, not evangelism. Apologies for the confusion.

This is the part where numerous readers say "don't judge others." Yes, it is hard not to look at others who make different choices than we do when it comes to serving. As long as you do a little good, it all comes out right in the end. I wrestle with this every day. I ask questions of myself like:

Have I done enough good today?

Did I make an impact for the kingdom today?

As I tried to explain their trip and our trip I honestly struggled. My heart judged them as not doing a good enough job in mission. Being very frustrated and judgmental of their group is not the way of Christ. They were doing a two day mission trip with a bunch of theme park thrown in. To this day I wish I had the words to celebrate their trip and our trip with my team. I failed.

Here is what ran through my mind as I tried to justify my own thoughts and feelings. It was obvious they were on a fun trip with some mission thrown in. Think about it, I mean, how much does it cost to drive, stay and go to a theme park? Thousands and thousands of dollars would be wasted. What if that was put to mission? Hey wait, don't make me feel bad about theme parks! I'm not, but when you raise money for "missions" and spend it on more fun than serving, it should cause all of us to question the motives. All of these words and views go against the work and will of God. Sanctimonious party of one, your table is ready. I'm guessing I might not be the only one judging them here. Stay with me, because we all could do some learning together.

It is easy to sit back and compare ourselves with others and feel as if we are better than them. We do this is so many ways. The words I now have, which I wish I had then, are amen and hallelujah! A group of teenagers traveling across the country to make a positive impact for Jesus Christ is something to be celebrated, not diminished. It's commendable these days when people take their time, resources and passion to serve one another. I do not excuse my lack of words and inability to frame their work in a positive light. Growth as a Christian is something we all need to do, every day. In the years since that experience I have grown and I am now able to celebrate both trips.

My goal here is to really have each of us examine the overall impact of serving one another. There are for sure good and bad ways to serve. Sometimes our mission trips can hinder the development and growth of others by not allowing people to grow in partnership. We should all be convicted to provide a long lasting positive impact for those we serve, while recognizing sometimes we are just one group following another group keeping a project going. Anyone willing to serve should be thanked and celebrated. Judging someone else's service is not terribly gracious and dare I say, it's not very Christian. When serving, consider the impact and the overall purpose. Are we serving so we feel better or are we serving to change the world for Jesus Christ? Easy answer here, but we should contemplate our service in the larger picture of the kingdom of God.

"Then he will say to those on his left, 'Depart from me, you who are cursed, into the eternal fire prepared for the devil and his angels. For I was hungry and you gave me nothing to eat, I was thirsty and you gave me nothing to drink, I was a stranger and you did not invite me in, I needed clothes and you did not clothe me, I was sick and in prison and you did not look after me.' "They also will answer, 'Lord, when did we see you hungry or thirsty or a stranger or needing clothes or sick or in prison, and did not help you?' "He will reply, 'Truly I tell you, whatever you did not do for one of the least of these, you did not do for me.' Matthew 25:41-45

Again, Ouch. No judgement here. Honestly, it pains me to say these things. I go back and forth even now as I write this, because, c'mon pastor, at least we are trying to make the world a better place. We are and I get it, but is there another way we could make a better more qualitative impact? Humbly I believe so, but I could be wrong here. What are we teaching our children and youth? They see how we spend our resources and what we care about, goodness gracious we can do better. Enough said. Let's leave this chapter with a warm fuzzy story.

Three Wise Guys

Inspiration comes in many forms. Sometimes you hear something on the radio, a pastor says something that clicks or a notion crosses your mind. How do we respond? Ignore? Listen? Act? Well, one such notion came around Thanksgiving and as we listened to God, we formulated a plan.

The church I serve has some of the most brilliant and amazing Christians I've ever met. They are faithful, selfless and up for a challenge. In our area there was a man known as the "Secret Santa." He would walk around and give money away to people he felt could use it. After he passed away, a few others have taken up the cause, but no one has truly impacted the way he did.

In our case, we decided to be known as the three wise guys. We obtained permission from local businesses to walk around and hand money to anyone we felt God was prompting us to give money to and the results were amazing. If you follow this path, please obtain permission because this kind of service can become disruptive. We pooled our resources and went out about town handing out cash. It was strange at first, but once you give to a few people, it becomes much easier. The response from those we encountered was humbling. Tears of joy, hugs and people unable to speak. You could call them random acts of kindness, but there was a prayerfully thought out, talked out and walked out plan.

Finally, there was one family that a wise guy knew that was in great need. She was a single mom of four who had been struggling the last year and he felt led to help. So, we dressed up in crazy Christmas outfits and delivered a Christmas meal, clothes, toys and money to her doorstep. Again, tears and she was unable to speak. The inspiration was heaven sent and the impact echoes through the kingdom of Heaven.

Do you know someone in need of help? Are you afraid to approach them and step up? If so, then do it anonymously. I can't count the number of people our church has helped through service and missions, and often anonymously. Church folks are changing the world by serving those in need, and they are doing it day by day and without a spotlight. Our family has made it part of our yearly goal planning to help those in need. We've served in numerous places that serve meals, donated to lots of causes and have tried to be ready to serve when needed. You can never do enough. There is always someone to help. You can't ever stop serving. Yes, you might feel exhausted, but your soul will be filled with joy.

At the end of our lives I pray that we leave a lasting legacy and impact of serving. To live a spiritually healthy life of service, we can focus on the following inspiration words.

"Do all the good you can,
By all the means you can,
In all the ways you can,
In all the places you can,
At all the times you can,
To all the people you can,
As long as ever you can."[6]

This is how we know what love is: Jesus Christ laid down his life for us.
And we ought to lay down our lives for our brothers and sisters. If anyone
has material possessions and sees a brother or sister in need but has no pity
on them, how can the love of God be in that person? Dear children, let us
not love with words or speech but with actions and in truth.

1 John 3:16-18

I look back over my short career in ministry and smile because I've seen so many people helped by the church. Every church usually has a focus on serving and helping others. Please consider supporting the church in her efforts. The impact of a large group of people on a mission for God can and will change the world. The church is the greatest force of good in this world and together, we will help end homelessness, food insecurity and radically reduce the poverty rate. It is our calling and passion to serve and make the biggest impact possible.

Chapter 7- Time, Resources and Passion

My mom makes the best fried chicken ever. Now that is saying something where I come from, because just about every restaurant and diner serve fried chicken around here. And I love good fried chicken. I prayed for years that God would provide a fast food fried chicken place in our community and hallelujah, my prayers were answered! Her fried chicken rivals any I've ever tasted. No one has anything on my mom's fried chicken. It's absolutely delicious. Apologies to all the moms out there who feel theirs is the best fried chicken. Feel free to send me the recipe or drop some by the church any time you want.

Mom's chicken is served with homestyle chicken gravy, mashed potatoes with extra butter and creamed corn. No bread or biscuit because there is not enough room on my plate. A symphony of flavors and smells bring smiles to all those who choose to enter the kitchen while she is cooking. It's crispy chicken, not fried and then steamed like so many farm kitchens serve. Nothing against fried and steamed, but crispy is my preference. Funny thing is though, that is how my mom used to make chicken, just like her mom. They would fry it and then steam it in the oven. Then she met and married my dad, who likes crispy fried chicken.

He made the somewhat fateful decision one day to say to my mom, "My mom's fried chicken is better. Can you cook it like she does?" I was thankfully not alive at this time, but the story has been recounted enough times I know it by heart. My father did not have another home cooked fried chicken dinner for a year. Take note husbands, rule number one, never compare your wife's cooking to your mom's. Although in this case, it actually worked out. My mom talked to grandma and learned how she made and the rest is history. It is now her recipe for cooking fried chicken.

My mom also makes several other homemade family favorites. I grew up eating many farm to table meals. Mom grew up on a farm in western Kansas, and much of what they ate was not purchased at a grocery store. It was grown or raised, then canned or butchered. It was the farm life in the middle part of the last century. Bread was homemade and served warm, with butter. If you've never had homemade bread served warm with butter, you have missed a blissful experience. Unless you are gluten free and then apologies.

Those homemade favorites are passed down recipes from generations past. Most of them are not found in cookbooks, as they are family recipes that are more art than measurements. You may find them scrawled out on index cards, otherwise known as recipe cards. Much of it has to do with the way things are cooked, like the pan sizes and time cooked while preparing other things. Don't ask anyone at the local grocery store in the meat department to cut out the wishbone. Nary a restaurant that I know of will serve a wishbone. They were not trained to do that, so they don't know how. My mom worked in a grocery store deli many years ago that did know how to cut out the wishbone piece, because it provided another piece of chicken for the family and incidentally, my favorite piece as a kid, and adult.

I've tried for years to duplicate that recipe. I know the ingredients, spices, the measurements and how to cut up the chicken. However, it never tasted the same. I tried and tried, but I just couldn't ever get it right. Something was missing. For a family that likes to cook, for the life of us, my wife and I could not figure out what was missing. Seasonings were correct. Even the cooking oil was correct, but we just could not figure it out. It was a mystery.

Life can be comical sometimes. We know the path to take and yet, our experience can be different than others who traveled the same path. When you look at your spiritual life, what is missing? We maybe have the shape and form of the faith, but we just don't feel like was have it all together. It's like our chicken recipe, it just doesn't seem to be perfect. It's a bit off.

Our faith is something that needs to be shaped and formed, specifically by and with God. To become the Christian we know that we are called to be, requires us to take a few moments every day to evaluate where we've been and where we are going. A daily examination of our intention, desire and hope reveals a great deal of whose path we are truly on. Is it our path? Is it the path of God? Or, is the path of the world? The prophet Isaiah tried to sum up our relationship with God by comparing us to clay.

Yet you, Lord, are our Father. We are the clay, you are the potter; we are all the work of your hand.   Isaiah 64:8

We are the work of God's hand. We are shaped and molded in His image. For that to happen, we need to allow God to work in our daily life. How? Put yourself in a position to be fruitful in your faith. That requires gathering in worship, Bible study and service. You should not and truly cannot do faith alone.

For it is by grace you have been saved, through faith — and this is not from yourselves, it is the gift of God — not by works, so that no one can boast. For we are God's handiwork, created in Christ Jesus to do good works, which God prepared in advance for us to do.   Ephesians 2:8-10

If we are God's handiwork as the good book says, how does His piece of art look these days? God saved us for His purpose, not ours. The grace of God has been showered upon us, even though we are terribly undeserving and unworthy. When God works in our daily life our priorities will shift to be His priorities.

To understand the life of a disciple, we must look at where we spend our time, resources and energy. How much time do we spend on things that don't truly matter? Have we become experts in areas that have no eternal value? Knowing the latest sports scores or political gossip does not make for a fruitful life. It means you have useless information filling up space in your heart, soul and mind. When referring to troubles or priorities, my grandma used to say, "will it matter in a hundred years?" A big picture perspective is often needed when planning days, week and months.

What do our calendars say about our spiritual lives? Your daily and weekly calendar will show you exactly where your commitments and priorities are leading you. We are all going somewhere and the destination is picked by our daily choices. Of course work takes up a significant portion of our week, as does sleeping. If you have kids or are a student, then school schedules are added in, plus all the extracurricular activities. Do you ever stop and think, what does this all mean? Why am I running like this? Because you chose to run that way. Yes, you chose to run that direction. There were maybe outside pressures, community and worldly pressure, but you choose your walk.

Do not feel guilty about the choice to run in the direction you are running. Now that you have become aware of the connection between your choices and your time, you may need to change it. This might be a difficult thing for many, because we want to be polite and neighborly. Goodness gracious we middle of the country folks are overly concerned with being polite. So to give up some of those purposeless commitments might cause some trouble or disruption for friends and family. If you remember, Jesus chased people out of temple who missed the point. Disruption is part of the Christian walk. Sit down with your calendar, family and friends and chart a new course of discipleship. You can do this, it just takes you saying yes to Jesus and no to the world.

We now move into the one section of the book where people struggle the most. What might that be, well you know, don't you. It's obvious if you ask around. The most difficult topic in the church these days is not death or infidelity, it's talking about money. There you go, skipping to the next chapter or closing the book. If you are still here, stick with me. No guilt or shame, just honest conversation.

You cannot tithe your time. It is not a substitute to a disciplined financial life. I've often wondered if someone tithes (10% of your income to the church) because they are disciplined, or did they tithe and become disciplined. Either way, those who tithe do not usually struggle with their finances. Hear that again, those who tithe do not usually struggle with their finances. A tithe is 10%, free and clear to your church. Do not change the tithe to 10% to charity. Give to other charities above your tithe. Do not shortchange God. Budget your money and follow through.

I'm not sure if you have a budget or a family budget, but you should seriously consider it. It can be immensely helpful to you, your family and your walk with Christ. What do our budgets say about our spiritual lives? Many families own too much, have too much debt and not enough savings. We spend too much and don't give enough. Life is not about the accumulation of resources or how much we can consume in one lifetime. It's about living a lasting spiritual legacy to span generations. Reread that again. It's about living a lasting, not leaving, legacy to span generations. If you are jammed up in debt and financial hardship, there is a way out. That way out is a choice. Talk to the church, not for a hand out but a hand up.

Do you know the number one reason for divorce? The number one reason for divorce is not infidelity, it's money problems. The stress introduced into a marriage by money problems is often too much for a marriage to bear. It is so sad that something that involves simple, strategic and daily choices would ruin a true blessing from God. Much of your spiritual life is setting up good and healthy guardrails in your life and marriage. Those guardrails keep you on the straight and narrow path of God. It's when we deviate from God's plan that we find ourselves struggling, lost and hurting.

Remember this: Whoever sows sparingly will also reap sparingly, and whoever sows generously will also reap generously. Each of you should give what you have decided in your heart to give, not reluctantly or under compulsion, for God loves a cheerful giver. And God is able to bless you abundantly, so that in all things at all times, having all that you need, you will abound in every good work.   *2 Corinthians 9:6-8*

Friends, you reap what you sow. For those who don't plant gardens or farm, that means if you do not plant, it will not grow. Sow means to plant and reap means harvest. You will harvest what you plant. If you plant nothing on behalf of God, what will you harvest? It's not under compulsion or guilt, it's a heart open to where God might be leading you. We are blessed in following the path of God. It's not about giving to get either, it's about actually following the disciplined life God has set before us. It's a choice to reject the way of the world and follow God. Ok, there you go. That is the end of the tithing discussion and hopefully, enough said.

Finally, where do we expend our energy? If you are more fired up about your local sports team than church, you might have an eternity problem. Was that too harsh? It felt a bit harsh, almost on the side of tough love. Now there's a phrase I don't want to get in the weeds with! An honest examination of our spiritual motives in regard to our passion can be embarrassing or even possibly painful. When you love someone you tell the truth, right? Honesty is the best policy. So let's walk into the passion issue that we so often suffer from in the church because isn't everyone just bored to death of church? Yes, excuses, excuses from one too many people would be that worship is boring. Again, what are you putting into it?

I've heard something like seventy to eighty percent of churches did not have new members or any baptisms last year. The church has a few problems, and sadly, passion is one of them. Some Christians have become bored so they change the style of their worship service. It's like we keep changing the design and colors on our soda can. Look at us, we are new and hip, just come hang out. Sorry, again, too harsh.

We are creatures that do like the new and fast. How come they make cars that exceed the speed limit by over one hundred miles per hour? Because they can, and we will buy it. Those speeds are neither sufficient or necessary, they just are and we will buy it. If we are on fire for Jesus then we don't chase after the way of the world. Some of the happiest, most fulfilled people I know live a modest lifestyle, with older cars and a sense of contentment that is rarely seen these days.

It's ok to be busy, but not for the world's sake. Strike a healthy balance, and make sure if you are not in weekly worship, you are in the "mission field" speaking well of your pastor and church. Passion is deeply connected to your heart, soul and mind. Jesus was once asked what was required to receive eternal life.

On one occasion an expert in the law stood up to test Jesus. "Teacher," he asked, "what must I do to inherit eternal life?" "What is written in the Law?" he replied. "How do you read it?" He answered, "'Love the Lord your God with all your heart and with all your soul and with all your strength and with all your mind'; and, 'Love your neighbor as yourself.'" "You have answered correctly," Jesus replied. "Do this and you will live." Luke 10:25-28

Do this and you will live. Eternal life is a gift freely given from God because of His love for us. Love is powerful. We are called to love God with our heart, soul, strength and mind. To love God means our focus is on His purpose, not ours. The recipe of the Christian is faith, hope and love. All three are ingredients that will help you find your passion again. Where is your faith? Where is your hope? What and who do you love? If your answer is your favorite sports team or a possession in your life, it's time to mix up your recipe of life because the world was added way too much into it.

Back to my story from earlier about struggling to complete the fried chicken recipe. It took us a few years, but we finally figured out what we were doing wrong with my mom's fried chicken. We had made two huge errors. Although they may not seem like much, they actually changed the final product enough that it came really close to her original recipe.

The first error we made was timing. If you ever watch a cook they trust that the heat and pan are working together and they don't check it every few minutes. In fact, they almost ignore what is cooking in the pan until they decide to check on it. If you sit in a kitchen and observe, there is rarely a timer, unless someone is baking a pie. Yum, pie. It's more of a feeling it's time to turn the chicken over in the skillet. Both of us kept checking on the chicken by removing the cover to see how it was cooking. This releases a bunch of the heat and steam so then it did not cook properly. You have to trust the process and learn when things are ready. Just like life, faith takes time. It's not an overnight thing. Being a disciple of Jesus takes years and years of disciplined work. That is not earning or working to receive salvation, it's a response to God giving us salvation. On our salvation journey we work for Him, not us.

The other error we made was we discounted the effect of the actual skillet. My mom has always used an electric skillet to cook chicken. She does not cook it on the stove in a pan like many other people do. We never had a gas stove either, so that meant no cast iron. The pan we were using was our stainless steel wedding present from my sisters to cook the chicken in, and it for sure did not taste the same. It was good, but not great. We thought our best pan would do, but it didn't. Don't assume the best, brightest, newest, shiniest thing is better than the way those before us did things. Often times, the new is a piece of junk that won't last but a few years. Wisdom is something accumulated over time and it's something that too many of us ignored in our younger years. Listen and respect your elders. They know more than they share because they are waiting for you to realize you don't know as much as you think you do. It took me a few years to figure that out.

"Therefore everyone who hears these words of mine and puts them into practice is like a wise man who built his house on the rock. The rain came

down, the streams rose, and the winds blew and beat against that house;
yet it did not fall, because it had its foundation on the rock. But everyone
who hears these words of mine and does not put them into practice is like a
foolish man who built his house on sand. The rain came down, the streams
rose, and the winds blew and beat against that house, and it fell with a
great crash."   Matthew 7:24-27

We had sadly built our chicken recipe on sand because we did
not pay attention to everything. Our attempt to duplicate was
poorly executed because we did not realize the recipe is more than
what's on the page. It's no different than the faith. To fully
understand our time, resources and passion, we must look to other
Christians. They have answers and paths we've never thought of
walking down. It's up to us to seek out their advice and hear about
their recipe's. They've been down this road before and they might
know a better way. Why continue to build our faith on sinking
sands of the world instead of the firm foundation of Jesus Christ?

Here is the real deal though: your recipe for the faith will not be
exactly like your parents or those who showed you the way, the
truth and the life. The faith you received will change, adapt and
grow. It's no different than our chicken recipe. It changed. We chose
to customize it to our likes and so the recipe is a bit different and it
may not be exactly the same, but it keeps the spirit of the original.
Ultimately, we can never go home again, but we have a new home
secured in heaven for all those who call on the name of the Lord.

Chapter 8- You Are the Light of the World

This is the verdict: Light has come into the world, but people loved darkness instead of light because their deeds were evil. Everyone who does evil hates the light, and will not come into the light for fear that their deeds will be exposed. But whoever lives by the truth comes into the light, so that it may be seen plainly that what they have done has been done in the sight of God.   *John 3:19-21*

My family loves to go camping. Wait, scratch that. My wife, kids and I like to go camping. My extended family tolerates our week long camping adventures. We rent cabins and put up tents, cook an amazing breakfast and spend time outside. Disc golf is a favorite activity, as is fishing and water balloons. Currently we have over twenty nieces and nephews on both sides. During our camping trips, we invite both sides.

It's a rarity that this happens in most families. For us though, it continues to build relationships with our two amazing families. Not everyone can attend our meet in the middle camping trips. Since I work on Sundays, we camp during the week, which means grandparents and those who live close are able to attend. College students and teens attend as well. It makes for a great week of family and fun. If you have never been out in nature camping or in a cabin, you have missed out. We like to stay on state land near a lake. The roads are paved for kids riding bikes, and there are very few people who take advantage of the area, so you basically have the place to yourself.

One year while tent camping we arrived before anyone else to set everything up and secure our sites. It was mid-week and no one was out where we were. The lake and the campsite were ours. It was peaceful. Living in a stressful high demand world, it's good to unplug and get away from it all. As we set up our tent and kindly and gently disagreed as to the "how", we felt wonderfully blessed. Ok, let's be honest. Two things will cause the best marriages and the best couples to fight. One of them is setting up a new tent for the first time. The directions are never clear and it shines a light on the absolute tragic nature of communication skills. The other thing that can cause communication issues in a marriage is canoeing.

If you have never been canoeing, you might rethink your desire to do so. We once canoed down a river in Arkansas. Communication skills and boating skills that are not honed and clear can make for some interesting conversations. You may not be aware, but the person in the back of the canoe "guides" or "steers" the canoe. The person up front usually provides a large portion of the power to move the canoe. So then if the person in the back of the canoe has no idea how to steer then you go in circles. It's funny the first time, but not after one hundred times on a humid day in August. However, it can teach you a lot about yourself and how you react to difficulty. It might be a good exercise in patience and love. We have been canoeing again, but not very often.

Back to us setting up the camp site. We brought our normal set of camping equipment that had been collected over the years. There is a tendency to make sure we bring anything and everything we might possibly need. We pack pretty tight and efficient when traveling, except when camping. Pots, pans and all other manner of camping accessory that we purchased, thinking it a necessity, is packed dutifully in our tubs. This provides for the perfect camping experience, only if the tubs are accurately labeled.

We spent the first night on the lake, with our tent twenty yards from the shore. There was a nice north wind that helped keep the waves coming in which made for a nice sound to help the weary camper sleep well. Around two in the morning I was startled awake by the sound of a truck driving in the distance. I sat up to hear it coming closer and closer. I reached for a flashlight to see what was going on. This was the middle of the week, we were the only ones on this campsite.

The area where we were camping was surrounded by water on three sides. We we were on the north side, the road ran east to west, and looped back to the main road. The truck drove down our loop and seemed to disappear. Being the middle of the night, I could not tell if I had dreamed it or what was going on. Of course, the fear of us being there alone crept into the back of my mind. What was one to do? And then I remembered my new camping gear I had just purchased for this trip. It was a spotlight that caught my eye and imagination at the local sports store.

Not completely sure of what had transpired, I grabbed my new spotlight and stepped outside the tent. This was no ordinary spotlight. It was a 2,000,000 candlepower spotlight. I have no idea what that means, but the sales pitch worked on me. As I walked away from the tent I felt less fear, knowing I had this amazing light in my hands. I felt confident that this light would blind anyone and would illuminate the whole area. I set up in what I thought was a strategic location as to where I thought the truck might have parked, if it had not exited the area yet.

I held up the light, pointed it west and flicked the on switch. It snapped to life and lit up the whole campsite. The immense power of this light did not disappoint. In that very moment, I felt vindicated in my impulse purchase. The light shone all around the campsite and revealed no nefarious activity. There was no sign of the truck and no sign of anything. The sheer power of this light in the middle of the night caused my more juvenile nature to spring out. I held the light to the sky and it looked as if I could land planes in our little campsite. After a few moments of joy, playing with my new toy, I retired to the tent with the assurance and confidence of safety because the darkness did not win and a powerful light was just a few feet away from me as I slept.

"I am the light of the world. Whoever follows me will never walk in darkness, but will have the light of life." John 8:12

When Jesus pronounced He was the light of the world a few religious leaders probably didn't appreciate it. Who was the upstart young Rabbi saying such things? How dare He proclaim to be the light! What did it even mean for them at that time? Light brings life and safety. It allows us to travel without darkness. Traveling at night could be treacherous and Jesus proclaiming to be the light meant you don't need to walk in darkness anymore. The I Am was here. Jesus has seven I Am statements in the Gospel of John. They are:

I Am The Bread of Life

I Am The Gate

I Am the Good Shepherd

I Am The Way, the Truth and the Life

I Am The Vine

I Am The Light of the World

I Am The Resurrection and Life

For a people that knew God as I Am, Jesus claiming all these things was startling. In the naming of His character we find a path shared for the believer to understand His true nature. We are sustained, cared for, shown the way and given new life. Doesn't every one in the world want these things? No, sadly they don't.

Take heart, Jesus has overcome the world. When you choose to believe and follow Jesus, His light is evident. It is revealed in how we walk the path. Your faith will carry the light into some of the saddest and darkest places.

The world is full of darkness. Some of our family and friends walk in darkness. We too sometimes walk in darkness. When we follow Jesus, the darkness fades away and we live in and into the light. You can see it, can't you? A fallen and broken world continues it's fits and fights as it gasps for relevance against a mighty and loving God. When the Israelites escaped Egypt a wonderful and beautiful image is shared in the Scriptures. It says they were led by a pillar of fire at night.

By day the Lord went ahead of them in a pillar of cloud to guide them on their way and by night in a pillar of fire to give them light, so that they could travel by day or night. Neither the pillar of cloud by day nor the pillar of fire by night left its place in front of the people.

Exodus 13:21-22

They were fleeing injustice, suffering and pain. The oppression they experienced had diminished their hope to such an extent it caused them to want to go back when they faced adversity. Imagine choosing to go back into an awful and abusive situation because the path to freedom was too hard. Too many these days feel as if there is no hope and their world can't get any better. Too many are unwilling to stand up and with others in the midst of their suffering and pain. Our politeness masquerades often as a barrier to real change and honest conversation. I'm speaking to myself here as well.

Jesus is the light of the world. He brings hope and joy to all who call on His name. Why would we not carry this message to the nations? How can we sit on this extraordinary and vital message of freedom from sin? Jesus is the trillion candle powered light of the world. He is a beacon of hope to the oppressed, the prisoner and the wounded. Yet, they will never know this if His people do not get out there and shine the light of Christ. What is it going to take for us to get out there and shine the light? Are we afraid? Go out and shine the light of Christ. Light your candle and touch the world. Let them know about a God who loves them, wants the best for them and can set them free. Jesus also said,

"You Are the light of the world"   Matthew 5:14

The church is the light of the world, but too often we bring guilt and shame. Here is a very practical way too look at shining the light of Christ. Do your words and deeds reflect the glory of the Lord? You see, one of the biggest complaints from non-believers about Christians is not Jesus, but how His believers conduct themselves. Amen to that. We hear they love Jesus, but not the church. Let's be honest, no they don't. They don't know Jesus and they don't know the church.

They have an idea or a notion about Jesus, but to really know Jesus means you have accepted Him as your Lord and Savior, not just His philosophical teachings. They may know the groovy peace and love Jesus, but not the believe, follow and discipleship version of Jesus. I am sure that the giving up your possessions to follow Jesus has not reached the masses. Some are horribly misinformed about Jesus. The church they think they know is messed up, full of hypocrites and sinners. Wait a minute, that's the church I serve as well. Hmm, so the world demands Christians are perfect, when we know we are not. So the non-believer concept of church isn't what we should strive for, meaning we shouldn't listen or chase after the crowds. Exactly. Shine your light, not the light the crowd desires.

That all sounds a bit harsh. Maybe it is and if so, feel convicted. We are not perfect, but at least we have the love of Jesus in our heart. It's difficult to hear criticism about the church from folks who don't really know the church or Jesus. Can we listen and maybe see things revealed we had not seen before? Yes. Do we chase after trends and relevancy by catering to a fallen and broken culture? No. Do not lose your integrity following after the world. The world is to be redeemed, not smoothed out or chipped away. Redemption requires a lot more than subtle changes.

Being the light of Christ means we need to be willing to share our gifts with others. The Holy Spirit has gifted you with something special. You are to share it to help transform the world for Jesus Christ. Shining the light leads us to bring the light with us, every where we go. So we must go and share the light. When and where do we go to share the light? Great question. Every where. Do not shine the light in judgment of others, but as a beacon to bring people closer to Jesus.

We are the light when we offer hospitality, service and no judgement. Imagine a church that truly does not judge people for what they have done, but is deeply concerned about where they are going. I've heard way too many stories of churches asking people to leave because they didn't fit in. They either had a past or didn't have the right look about them. Jesus weeps friends, He weeps when His church fails to shine the light. An open church, welcoming of all sinners is the best way to go. Who am I, who are you to say who is in and who is out? Don't ever think it's your call, it's not. It is truly and only in the hands of God.

That leads me to a wonderful and spectacular word known as Grace. Ah, the grace of God. Grace is the absolutely unmerited favor of God. We don't earn it, buy it or trade for it. It is God revealing the divine nature to us in forgiveness and love. We are called to offer that grace to others because we have been offered it. Grace says it's ok to not be perfect. Grace allows us to grow together and closer to God. One of the greatest struggles in the church and life is allowing others to grow and change. As the light of God moves you closer to Him you will change. Just like our garden, the light changes things.

There are groups of people all over the world that are warning the population about artificial light pollution. Essentially, as urban and suburban areas grow, we will be unable to see the stars in the night sky because there is too much artificial light. The maps and predictions are a bit alarming. I grew up in the country and we were always able to see the stars in the sky. If something is not changed soon, young kids will grow up and never see the stars of the sky unless they travel far from the city.

It's telling that we often trade convenience for the things that really matter. Sometimes it's not a conscious choice, and we do not consider the consequences of our choices and behavior. In the life of the Christian, we will often trade the light of Christ for the artificial lights of the world. What do I mean here? The artificial lights of this world trick you into believing you are fulfilled and happy, only to see your life come crashing down around you because of false idols, broken relationships and the wrong road taken.

Awareness is key to choose the real light of Jesus over the false light of the world. If we are unaware of the sin in us we can never change. It's not about guilt or shame, but acknowledging and choosing the light of Jesus in every word and every deed. The world will tempt us and pull us in every direction except the way of Christ. Give yourself permission to make a few mistakes along the way, but once you are aware of the true path, take it! No backsliding please because life is too short and too precious. Our friends, family and neighbors could already be living a life estranged from God because they follow the artificial light. That light only temporarily masks our sin and struggle, but in the end, we will be broken and lost. Do not let yourself be led down that path and I implore you to fight for those walking the wrong road. Don't fight with them, fight for them!

My two million candle powered spotlight was a thing of beauty. It was impressive. Of course, the need for new and better caused the market to replace my spotlight. The most powerful spotlight was replaced a few years later with the three million and I'm sure it will continue to be replaced with brighter spotlights. You can keep trading up for more powerful and artificial lights, or you can follow the true light of the world. As I said before, it's a daily choice which light to follow.

The light changes our perspective on things and will radically change your heart if you are open to it. When one has seen the light, it implies there was darkness before and now it's gone. God is the light, and now we are the light of Christ. That light will not burn out and it should not be hidden. Where do you need to shine the trillion candle powered light of Jesus? Who is suffering and who is lost these days? It may be a beacon in the midst of your loved one's storm, so shine that light! Shine it every day you walk this earth and help bring everyone home safe.

Chapter 9- Preach the Word, Share the Faith

When I was a young minister, I was naive. Ignorance is bliss in ministry and it keeps you from worrying about every little thing in the church and it causes you to try some outrageous things to reach people for Jesus Christ. I assumed the purpose of the church was to make disciples of all nations and that means you actually, wait for it, talk to strangers. So, full of passion and the Spirit I suggested to the churches I was serving that we invite people that live around the building to Sunday worship. The blank stares back at me led me to a new understanding I had not known. Some church people are afraid to talk to strangers. I also recently learned, many pastors are afraid to talk to strangers as well.

Many years ago the church had a model for inviting people to church and it was known as FRAN. Invite your friends, relatives and neighbors. It was quite popular and often repeated in sermons, newsletters and bulletins. However, the new evangelistic program was not terribly successful. Why you might ask? Most Christians struggle to invite people to church, let alone talk to people about their faith. Notice I used the word "most." Some Christians will share the faith and invite people to church worship services. Even a few will actually witness and help people be led to a relationship with Jesus Christ. Most. Some. Few.

Jesus went through all the towns and villages, teaching in their synagogues, proclaiming the good news of the kingdom and healing every disease and sickness. When he saw the crowds, he had compassion on them, because they were harassed and helpless, like sheep without a shepherd. Then he said to his disciples, "The harvest is plentiful but the workers are few. Ask the Lord of the harvest, therefore, to send out workers into his harvest field." Matthew 9:35-38

Near one of the churches I used to serve was a trailer park. It was less than a mile up a hill and was populated with around fifteen to twenty trailers. So, with a stack of door hangars, I convinced some youth and parents to go hang fliers on doors and invite people to Easter services. It was fun. As a big group, we did not feel alone or fearful. We had a purpose. A holy purpose indeed. As we walked and talked with people, several hearts melted and a few people accepted our invitation.

Over the next few weeks some of our neighbors showed up in worship. They brought their children, youth and grandchildren. When I think back on this experience my eyes well up knowing that for that moment, the church went outside the walls and invited people to meet Jesus. The folks that came built relationships with the church and became the church. Strong, faithful and life long ties were made in those weeks before and after Easter. Those new families found their pews and a place in the kingdom.

I don't think Jesus knew a stranger. He talked to all kinds of people. Jesus broke down barriers between tribes, groups and people with conversation. Let me say that again, Jesus talked to people. He ate with sinners, talked to Samaritans and in general stirred up the religious class. Not a bad thing for a thirty something year old Rabbi with a rag tag band of followers. One specific encounter gets at the heart of his message.

When a Samaritan woman came to draw water, Jesus said to her, "Will you give me a drink?" (His disciples had gone into the town to buy food.) The Samaritan woman said to him, "You are a Jew and I am a Samaritan woman. How can you ask me for a drink?" (For Jews do not associate with Samaritans.) Jesus answered her, "If you knew the gift of God and who it is that asks you for a drink, you would have asked him and he would have given you living water." "Sir," the woman said, "you have nothing to draw with and the well is deep. Where can you get this living water? Are you greater than our father Jacob, who gave us the well and drank from it himself, as did also his sons and his livestock?" Jesus answered, "Everyone who drinks this water will be thirsty again, but whoever drinks the water I give them will never thirst. Indeed, the water I give them will become in them a spring of water welling up to eternal life." John 4:7-14

Living water is like a spring that wells up inside of us to eternal life. Jesus talks to a woman that His own religious customs would outlaw and their practice would cause the avoidance of such people. But here is Jesus, breaking down walls and barriers to tell people about eternal life and the gift of God. This is a beautiful and perfect moment in His ministry. At the end of this encounter the disciples show up and do not question Him or ask why He was talking to her. Were they fearful to engage Him because their own customs and views would need to change?

The church is sometimes rather inwardly focused. We hang out with the same folks, sit in the same pews or chairs every week and that is ok. Let me say that again, it's ok to hang out with the same people. We also need to care enough about guests, visitors and new believers to move beyond our comfort zone and connect with them. An invite to lunch with new folks might be helpful as they find their way in the church. All you need to do is ask or invite.

I often wonder what it would be like to try and fit into a new church. I've been a pastor for around twenty years. I've served in several different churches over that time, but only once had an experience of attending a "new" church, but I didn't go in cold. I knew some people and felt welcomed. An invitation had been issued and I accepted. Even though I went alone, I ran to into some other people I knew and it was a really good time. However, I only went a few times. The preaching, band and fellowship were all good, but it was a long drive and I just didn't feel that motivated to stay connected.

Many in the church feel this way today. Church has become boring to many, and often times some Christians just don't feel motivated to attend or connect. Truthfully, they are weary, worn out and radically distracted by the world. We all sense it and feel it. As the culture continues to slouch in a direction away from God, some nominal Christians have now become nominal atheists. So, the response has become turning church into something unrecognizable to many Christians. I'm not sure if that is a good or bad thing. I have lots of questions. Questions are good, especially if those around you will engage in healthy and holy conversation. I have no idea how to deal with the struggles of churches losing in attendance and membership. I can say that when a church loses focus on it purpose of making disciples, it will struggle and eventually die. For every new vision or plan we've tried to compete with the world, the simple truth is we need to better connect with our community and invite people to really follow Jesus Christ. Enough said.

The church has a tendency to feel like you are attending someone else's family reunion. Sometimes family reunions can be great, mostly for the food, fellowship and possibly the music. Other times, you see two of your relatives go at it over past wrongs, politics or sports. I've heard screaming matches from the church kitchen and just shook my head in disbelief. We Christians sure do bottle up a bunch of stuff under the surface and service. God help the frightful guest entering our slice of heaven on a Sunday morning when so and so are being "who they are."

Not so long ago some friends moved to a new town. If you've ever moved to a new town, one of the ways to find out what is going on is learning what the town celebrates. What does that mean? Nearly every town in America has a festival or event that is "the" event of the year. They pour massive amounts of time, resources and energy into pulling off the event. People from surrounding communities will attend the event. It takes on a life of it's own. Rarely does anyone except the town historians remember who started it, but we keep gathering and celebrating. They have names like the "Wheat Festival", "Maple Leaf Festival" or the "City Wide Picnic."

Many of these events turn into several day affairs. Contests are added to the overall event to bring in the young folks. Maybe a parade and carnival rides are added as well. Civic organizations will join in offering a variety of booths, food and events. There are those few brave souls that work tirelessly to pull off the perfect event and they are often under-recognized and just do it for the community. Their amazing sacrifice and efforts are rarely noticed until they are gone. My friends experienced this first hand.

As they moved to the new community they heard from the realtor and neighbors about the community festival. It started the first day with a fun run, followed by a series of other events all over town and culminated with a big city wide evening celebration. My friend relayed to me after the event that he had the odd experience of being a complete outsider. He knew no one but wanted to make the best of it by joining in the activities.

He signed up for the fun run. The day of the event they had the usual town speakers listing off the sponsors and purpose of the event. It was all noise to him until this phrase came across speaker's lips, "And we all need to remember and be thankful for Stella⁷. She loved this festival and we appreciate her hard work." My friend thought that it was nice they thanked one of the organizers in such a big way. Over the next few days he continued to hear about Stella and her amazing and faithful work and how hard the festival was to put on. At the end of three days he was asking "Who in the world is Stella?"

After finally asking around, he learned she was a town saint who had organized the event for a long time. She had inherited leadership for the event from her mom and Stella hoped she could pass it on to the next generation some day. Stella had passed away before this year's event and the town organizers realized how little they had done to help. Frankly, they were ashamed and in posthumous posterity they lifted her name high. Who knew what the festival would be like from now on, but no one could fill Stella's shoes. The organizers managed to pull off a pretty good event, but it took several people doing the work of one Stella.

I'm not a big fan of lone rangers in ministry. They burn out, end up bitter and frustrated. Shooting stars burn bright and eventually flame out. The church needs to collaborate and work together to reach others for Jesus Christ. We are better together, not alone. Often times it's easier to go it alone. We've all been there in the church, haven't we? An event is planned and we jump in to help, only to become weary and we wonder why do we keep doing this? When I left youth ministry I was pretty burned out. Like many before, I shouldered most of the load for the ministry and overworked myself. The church was not solely to blame for that, I was too. We all need to take more accountability for our time and be fully aware if we begin to lose our passion.

Poor Stella did so much for her community they had no idea how little they were all contributing. Maybe she was tough to work with, or maybe she didn't want help. Either way, we all need to step up and help out. You can't leave all the work to one or two people. The numbers quoted to me since I began ministry are that twenty percent of the people do eighty percent of the work. We can and should do better. We are called by Jesus to go make disciples of all nations. It can't be just your pastor or you. Don't assume someone else will take care of making disciples. As my wife often says, "we are all in this together", so let's act like it.

Let me ask you a big question. Is your pastor Stella? If you don't have a pastor yet, let me explain. As I've consulted and mentored pastors these last few years, a common theme has come up. Most of them end up as building managers instead of pastors. Whether it's a parsonage or church, many have become plumbers, secretaries, audio visual experts, web site designers, marketers and a whole host of other duties that take away from their time to preach the Gospel and invite people to church. Way too many times I have heard and seen pastors toiling away on a project that moves them off mission. This leads to disillusionment and burnout. A number of pastors burn out every year and quit, not because they don't love Jesus. They love Jesus but struggle spiritually and emotionally with the ups and downs of church. The rollercoaster of ministry can take a toll on all of us. A lot of them feel as if the weight of the world is on their shoulders and they feel isolated and alone.

So, how can we keep our pastors and friends from becoming wrapped up in major events by themselves? First, recognize the problem. Identify it. Claim it and name it. Then deal with it. Set aside some time to volunteer at the church where you are most connected. If you are not connected to a specific church, volunteer at all of them. Spend three to five hours a week serving the church with the gifts God has given you. Don't worry, the kingdom is much bigger than a denomination or non-denomination. The kingdom needs servants and that servant is you!

The Apostle Paul, who wrote around thirteen letters in the New Testament, had a young pastor he was training. He offered advice to Timothy in a couple of letters. In one of them, he gives Timothy a direction for ministry.

Preach the word! Be ready in season and out of season. Convince, rebuke, exhort, with all longsuffering and teaching. For the time will come when they will not endure sound doctrine, but according to their own desires, because they have itching ears, they will heap up for themselves teachers; and they will turn their ears away from the truth, and be turned aside to fables. But you be watchful in all things, endure afflictions, do the work of an evangelist, fulfill your ministry. 2 Timothy 4:2-5

Not everyone will listen to you. That doesn't mean you don't invite. Whether it's a trailer park or a woman at the well, you go and you preach. Don't worry about the scoffers and people who reject you, focus on the people who say yes. Jesus told the disciples to shake the dust off their feet, which is a phrase not common to our time. In other words, shake it off. Let it go. Don't worry, be happy.

However, there are times when we invite and people show up and then they encounter "church people". God help us. One such occasion I invited a single mom and her daughter to church. They lived two houses down from the church, and on our side of the block there were only two houses. There was the church, church parking lot, parsonage and their house. Mom and daughter had only lived there for a few years and had never been invited to church. I invited them.

They showed up one Sunday and came in the wrong door. If you've been in a small church, you know there is always a wrong door. Anyway, they landed in the basement, below the sanctuary. With no signs where to go they approached a church member to ask for help. The response was classic insider church. Before the visitor could speak this lovely church member rudely said, "What are you doing here?" Remember this was a single mom with child in tow who lived two houses down. Shocked and surprised at the reception, she recounted her invitation from me and fortunately she was eventually shown the way upstairs to the sanctuary.

We can work so hard at the faith and have bad experiences. One person can cause us to be badly churched. You cannot and must not dwell on those experiences. None of us are perfect, we all make mistakes. The church is not immune from mean people. All too often the church puts them in leadership. The majority of Christians are kind, loving and caring people who want to make a difference in the world. They are doing their best to navigate the hectic world we live in. We have very few rules at the church I serve but one of them applies here. If you are mean to other people you cannot and will not be allowed to be in leadership. That sounds so simple, but many a church has allowed bullies and mean people to destroy the purpose and potential of the church.

Preach the word and share the faith. Look for the people around you without an invitation. They are right around the corner waiting to be asked. Reach out in concern and service to the world. They are waiting. You never know, you might change the enteral destination of your neighbor, a loved one or an enemy. It's all in how you react and respond to all that comes at you. Fulfill the calling on your heart. Always be conscious of the new folks in church and life. You can tell they are new by their mannerisms and behavior. We were all new once as well. Welcome them with the peace of Christ.

Chapter 10- Saved by the Bell

*After the Sabbath, at dawn on the first day of the week, Mary Magdalene
and the other Mary went to look at the tomb. There was a violent
earthquake, for an angel of the Lord came down from heaven and, going to
the tomb, rolled back the stone and sat on it. His appearance was like
lightning, and his clothes were white as snow. The guards were so afraid of
him that they shook and became like dead men. The angel said to the
women, "Do not be afraid, for I know that you are looking for Jesus, who
was crucified. He is not here; he has risen, just as he said. Come and see the
place where he lay. Then go quickly and tell his disciples: 'He has risen
from the dead and is going ahead of you into Galilee. There you will see
him. Now I have told you.* Matthew 28:1-7*

We all have irrational fears. We do. They creep up on us when we
least expect it. Some of us fear the dark, spiders, or public speaking.
Most of those things won't kill you, but it feels like it. One of my
irrational fears is being buried alive. I don't know where this fear
came from, maybe a movie or book, but it's real. It does not keep me
up at night, but every now and then, a chill runs down my spine
when I think of being buried alive.

Fear grips you. It does.

You might be reading this saying, that is completely irrational.
No one is buried alive these days, and you might be right. However,
I've done some research, and before the 1900's, people were
sometimes buried alive. How do we know this? Well, let's just say
there is ample evidence to the fact. In response to the rash of people
being buried alive, in the 1800's someone designed a safety coffin.

What is a safety coffin? There were numerous versions of safety coffins, but the one that catches my imagination is the one with a bell. Yes, you read it, a bell. If you had the unfortunate experience of being buried alive and your family spent the extra money on a safety coffin, a string was tied around your finger, which led up a tube, to a bell. So you could literally ring the bell and someone would save you. Hence, you could be saved by the bell.

Our fears keep us from being the people God needs us to be. Throughout life we are destined to face our fears. Whatever fears you have, you will face most of them. I've sat with families that faced their worst fears. Death is real and comes too often and too early. It is a constant that everyone knows about, but few face it until it's too late. There is a date in the future that holds our death. And when we go, we better have lived the life God placed before us. And hopefully, you won't be buried alive.

We know that Jesus Christ was not buried alive. He died on a cross, between two thieves. The guards pierced His side to make sure Jesus was dead. He had died. His body was taken down from the cross, prepared for burial and buried. A borrowed tomb was used for Him. A stone was rolled in front of His tomb so that His body could not be taken away by the disciples.

Jesus lay dead for three days. There were no windows, no light, just darkness. Jesus Christ, the Messiah and King of the Jews was dead. The tomb represented complete and utter failure for His disciples. They had walked with Him, learned from Him and had seen miracles. Others had been saved, others had been raised from the dead, but Jesus did not save Himself.

The hope of the disciples and other followers of Jesus was buried in the tomb with Him. His followers scattered out of fear of suffering the same fate. They hid from the world, worried they might die like Jesus. A locked door kept them safe from the world. It kept them safe from the their fears and worries, but not their sadness. Hope had died. Love had died. Their faith had apparently died too.

What the world had seen was the death of a peasant Rabbi, some prophet that was causing problems. His followers thought He was the son of God, the Messiah. Their greatest worries and fears were realized on the cross. The disciples failed Jesus. Their faith failed them. Then, everything changed. On a Sunday morning, the stone was rolled back and Jesus Christ was resurrected from the dead.

The angel said to the women, "Do not be afraid, for I know that you are looking for Jesus, who was crucified. He is not here; he has risen, just as he said. Come and see the place where he lay. Then go quickly and tell his disciples: 'He has risen from the dead and is going ahead of you into Galilee. There you will see him. Now I have told you.

Matthew 28:5-7

The angels said "do not be afraid." Yes. Amen. Hallelujah! No need to fear anymore, Jesus defeated the power of death. He has risen!!! As such, every human being on earth may receive the gift of eternal life and defeat the power of death. Amen.

The disciples then heard about this and ran to the tomb. They saw it empty, and most of them believed. Their Messiah was no longer dead, He was alive. Mourning turned to rejoicing, their sorrow to hope and their misery to joy. No need to fear anymore, because their Savior, the Son of God, the Messiah had won victory over the grave. The world did not win. The tomb did not win. Sadness, misery and lostness did not win. Jesus had won. God won. Those who choose to call on His name won. And yet, in hearing and knowing all those things, there are people in this world that still live in darkness, misery and sadness. Jesus was resurrected from the grave two thousand years ago. Billions of people profess the name of Jesus and people still have heartache and suffering. Why is that? Why O Lord, why?

We know them, don't we. They are our friends, family and neighbors. People are caught in darkness, misery and sadness. The church or Jesus have very little meaning in their lives. You might hear them say, I am spiritual, but not religious. Well, Jesus was amazingly religious and devout in His words and deeds. If we want to be like Him, then we need stop allowing people, even us, from making excuses.

Too many people today have buried themselves in a spiritual tomb of darkness. A wrong turn or a poorly lit path has put them in a place of darkness, sadness and misery. When someone falls in a pit it's difficult to dig their way out. They need help, not advice or judgement. If you witness someone fall down do you laugh at them or help them up? It probably depends on the someone.

Sadly, church folks tend to judge them for their bad decisions. Someone is in a pit and you think these words

"You made your bed, you need to lie in it."

"You made your grave, lie in it!"

We dismiss and judge people for their bad choices. They don't deserve it. A bad choice was made, a wrong turn was taken, but they don't deserve our judgement. The righteous stand on our pedestal from on high, judging and casting people out into the darkness. Continually pointing out someone's faults is a good way to keep them from a deep relationship with you. Love builds healthy relationships, not judgment and scorn.

Our job is not to judge but to figure out how to help them break free from the spiritual tomb of darkness. If someone asks you for directions you hopefully help. If they are lost, you tell them the way. Imagine a lost traveler stopping you and admitting they are horribly lost and they need some help. Your response, well, you got yourself into the mess you need to figure it out yourself. That is what the church often says to "sinners" and those caught in a life of misery and sin. What would Jesus do in that situation? He would point people in the right direction and maybe He might just walk with them.

We are called to bring the light of Christ into that situation. The light will show them a new path and the way home. Think about the people in your life right now that are dying a spiritual death. Yes they made some bad choices, and those choices were a free gift from God. You have the knowledge and path to salvation that will free them from their suffering, what are you going to do?

They rolled a stone in between them and God. It was rolled between them and anyone spiritual. Their excuses stink and are piling up one by one. Their lives are built around the seasonal, sporting and cultural events of their community, not Jesus and not the church. As the artificial lights slowly draws them further from God our response cannot be judging them. Judging others is condemning them, not saving them. I admit, it is a lot easier to condemn people and move on. We shake the dust off our feet and move on, but the church needs to at least try to reach them. The church is you, your family of believers and those gathered together in the name of Jesus.

The spiritual tomb of their own making is full of darkness, sadness and misery. Horrible mistakes led them to be buried alive and now they sit there waiting to be rescued. They distract themselves as best as they can, but they know they are lost. Some are offended by being told they are lost, whether it be spiritually or when traveling. Admitting that we are lost sets us down the path of redemption. The church must be a guide down that path. The previous barriers of judgement and criticism are not helpful when people seek the light.

Your faith needs to shine and point them in the right direction. The disciples of Jesus Christ struggled with this.

"Master," said John, "we saw someone driving out demons in your name and we tried to stop him, because he is not one of us." "Do not stop him," Jesus said, "for whoever is not against you is for you."

Luke 9:49-50

Jesus clearly explains here that if someone is working for the kingdom of God that we should not stop them because they are doing it differently. Think of how many churches think their way is the only true way. I think there will be some people in Heaven that we didn't expect to see there. Fortunately, God is in charge of that, not us. We don't get to decide who is in and who is out, and thank God!

As the time approached for him to be taken up to heaven, Jesus resolutely set out for Jerusalem. And he sent messengers on ahead, who went into a Samaritan village to get things ready for him; but the people there did not welcome him, because he was heading for Jerusalem. When the disciples James and John saw this, they asked, "Lord, do you want us to call fire down from heaven to destroy them?" But Jesus turned and rebuked them.

Luke 9:51-55

Wow. So if people don't welcome the church we should call down fire on them? That is what the disciples wanted to do to people opposed to them. First they wanted to stop people who were freeing people from spiritual darkness, then punish unbelievers. Jesus response to all of this is to rebuke the disciples. In others words, "get behind me Satan." They miss the point and so do we.

There are people right now ringing a bell in the spiritual tomb of their own making. They are buried because of the sin-filled choices and bad mistakes. The bell is ringing, what will the church do? Too often we will judge them or even ignore the sound of the bell. Cries for help are going unheard and we just turn up the band a bit louder to drown them out. Church, the world needs Jesus. It needs the light of Christ that will bring hope to the nations. For those struggling to find a meaningful relationship with God, they need you.

Our response cannot be judging them, we need to go to them. Break open the tombs that hold too many captive. Roll those stones away and go into that darkness. To roll the stone away takes two to three Christians, as it's a heavy stone and you do not want to go alone. Walk into the darkness and drag them out. Carry them out and deliver them into the light. Stop judging and start rescuing. Break down that stone and go get them. Just go!

When rescued, they will not be perfect. They will have questions and lots of doubts. We are called to help people meet Jesus, walk with Jesus and make it home. Spend lots of time walking with the new believer, helping them understand their life in Christ. Lead Bible studies and pray for them. Become a spiritual mentor and show them the way, the truth and the life. Be an example to your family, church and community. Shine the light of Christ in every word and in every deed. We all need to be the kind of Christians that demonstrate the fruit of the Spirit. What is the fruit of living in Jesus?

But the fruit of the Spirit is love, joy, peace, forbearance, kindness, goodness, faithfulness, gentleness and self-control. Against such things there is no law. Those who belong to Christ Jesus have crucified the flesh with its passions and desires. Since we live by the Spirit, let us keep in step with the Spirit. *Galatians 5:22-25*

Keep in step with the Holy Spirit. Do not judge, just rescue. Break open those spiritual tombs and help people. Bring the hope and joy of Jesus to the world. We live in a dramatically fallen and broken world, it needs Jesus Christ. People are buried alive in spiritual tombs of their own making, let's get up and get out there.

When Jesus got up and walked out of that tomb He declared victory over the darkness. His victory defeated sin, misery and death. We now all can receive the gift of salvation because He got up. Death o death where is your victory? Jesus defeated death and rose from the grave. Jesus is no longer on the cross. He is no longer in the tomb. He is alive forevermore. He got up. If not us, then who? If not now, when?

Notes

1. Blaise Pascal, *Pensées*. trans. A.J. Krailsheimer (London: Penguin Books. 1966, 1995) 121-127

2. Henry Knight III. and F. Douglas Powe, *Transforming Evangelism: The Wesleyan Way of Sharing the Faith*. (Nashville: Discipleship Resources. 2010), 15

3. The Lord's Prayer, *The United Methodist Hymnal* (Nashville: United Methodist Publishing House. 1989), 895

4. The Apostles' Creed, *The United Methodist Hymnal* (Nashville: United Methodist Publishing House. 1989), 881

5. Tony Jones, *The Teaching of the Twelve: Believing and Practicing the Primitive Christianity of the Ancient Didache Community*. (Brewster: Paraclete Press 2009), 18

6. This is a Methodist phrase in common use, but there is some dispute as to whether John Wesley ever said these words.

7. Name changed.